OLD TESTAMENT
PROPHETS
FOR TODAY

Also Available in the For Today Series:

OLD TESTAMENT PROPHETS FOR TODAY

Carolyn J. Sharp

WESTMINSTER
JOHN KNOX PRESS
LOUISVILLE • KENTUCKY

Book design by Sharon Adams
Cover design by Eric Walljasper, Minneapolis, MN

First edition
Published by Westminster John Knox Press
Louisville, Kentucky

This book is printed on acid-free paper that meets the American National Standards Institute Z39.48 standard. ∞

PRINTED IN THE UNITED STATES OF AMERICA

11 12 13 14 15 16 17 18 — 10 9 8 7 6 5 4 3 2

Library of Congress Cataloging-in-Publication Data

Sharp, Carolyn J.
  Old Testament prophets for today / Carolyn J. Sharp.—1st ed.
      p. cm.—(For today)
  Includes bibliographical references.
  ISBN 978-0-664-23178-1 (alk. paper)
  1. Bible. O.T. Prophets—Introductions.   I. Title.
  BS1505.52.S53   2009
  224'.061—dc22

                                                    2008033219

Contents

For Dinah and Jacob

Series Introduction

*T*he For Today series is intended to provide reliable and accessible resources for the study of important biblical texts, theological documents, and Christian practices. The series is written by experts who are committed to making the results of their studies available to those with no particular biblical or theological training. The goal is to provide an engaging means to study texts and practices that are familiar to laity in churches. The authors are all committed to the importance of their topics and to communicating the significance of their understandings to a wide audience. The emphasis is not only on what these subjects have meant in the past but also on their value in the present—"For Today."

Our hope is that the books in this series will find eager readers in churches, particularly in the context of education classes. The authors are educators and pastors who wish to engage church laity in the issues raised by their topics. They seek to provide guidance for learning, for nurture, and for growth in Christian experience.

To enhance the educational usefulness of these volumes, Questions for Discussion are included at the end of each chapter.

We hope the books in this series will be important resources to enhance Christian faith and life.

The Publisher

1

What Is a Prophet?

Who are the biblical prophets? Are their words relevant to us today? For some believers, everything in Scripture is worthy of deep and prayerful reflection: the Word of God never goes out of date! But others may not be so sure that a handful of prophets who lived in a preindustrial society 2,500 years ago have much to teach us. The prophets think they see God—but psychiatrists would tell us that Ezekiel's mystical chariot vision was a hallucination related to psychosis or post-traumatic stress disorder resulting from the prophet's experience of exile. The prophets think they speak for God—but social anthropologists would tell us that Jeremiah's counsel of submission to the invading Babylonian army reflects a predictable survival strategy of colonized people who face assimilation or death. The prophets think they know God. Well, that claim might compel our attention. Have you known the power of the sacred in your own life? Have you had an experience of God's love enfolding you when you were overwhelmed with grief? Have you come to sudden clarity while struggling in prayer to discern your way forward? Have you felt the energizing presence of the Holy Spirit in worship?

If so, then you know that God can surprise us by speaking through unexpected witnesses. Perhaps prophets from long ago can tell us something about God that we do not know. Perhaps they can tell us the truth about ourselves.

Truth-telling seems rarer and rarer these days. Every night when we watch the evening news, our perspectives are shaped by sophisticated media "spin" and the relentless manipulation of advertising. Truth is so often commodified and repackaged to meet the agendas of those in power, those with something to sell, and those who need to be needed. North American broadcast journalism has moved away from the paternalistic model of a single trusted anchorman telling us everything we need to know. The measured tones of the beloved Walter Cronkite have yielded to lively debates on television, radio, and Internet sites among many analysts, consultants, and opinion brokers.

This is generally a good thing. To be sure, technology can enable the dissemination of false information, and it makes possible the exploitation of far larger numbers of people than would have been possible before our global age. But technology can make the plight of a needy person or the riches of a faraway culture vividly present to a remote viewer; it can educate, and it is a powerful tool for fostering collaboration. Technology has made possible an electronic forum for Bible study that I lead: I can discuss Scripture and spiritual formation with dozens of people who would not normally show up for a Bible study at church. Technology can be a blessing.

But the play of many different perspectives may leave us wondering exactly where we may find truth. The proliferation of technologies for global public conversation—news, infotainment, reality shows, Facebook, YouTube, Webcasts—means that a dizzying number of analysts can claim authority in our cultural space. We are inundated with stories that are impossible to verify. Rumors fly at the speed of light. Political reputations are made or destroyed in a matter of days rather than years. Plagiarism flourishes as preachers and writers appropriate Internet-based materials as their own. Poorly formulated opinions and misinformation are rife on blogs and other Web sites. More than ever, we need guidance to discern what is true.

Here, the prophet can help. For the prophet is a truth teller. Whether we are comfortable with the prophetic voice or not, we sense that when the prophet speaks, truth is on offer. And the richest literary source about prophets in the cultural heritage of Western civilization is the Old Testament. This book invites you to explore the gifts that the Old Testament prophets can offer to us and to the church.

Who Is the Old Testament Prophet?

The Old Testament prophet is a compelling figure in the spiritual imagination of ancient Israel, the Christian church, and secular culture. Prophets are known in biblical memories from Israel's earliest times, when Abram was called from Mesopotamia and became the father of all who believe in Israel's God, to New Testament times. Clearly, the witness of the biblical prophets was taken seriously, for it has been preserved in stories, oracles, and collections of prophetic material throughout the Hebrew Scriptures. The prophetic voice thunders through Israel's culture early and late.

Israelite prophets respond to domestic economic, social, and cultic issues. They also respond to international crises involving military aggression against Israel by the Assyrians, the Babylonians, and other military powers (Egypt, Syria, and smaller nation-states such as Ammon, Edom, Tyre, and Philistia). The prophets were many things to the ancient Israelites, who by turns honored them and ignored them. Some within ancient Israel mocked the prophets as troublemakers; others treasured their witness and carefully preserved their words for future generations. Some scorned the prophets as deluded; others recognized that the prophetic word was the only reliable source of clarity in times of political turbulence and social anxiety.

For the Christian church, Israelite prophecy pointed to Christ. Many prophetic texts in the Hebrew Scriptures were understood by early Christian interpreters to foretell Christ's incarnation, ministry, suffering and death, or resurrection. Christian tradition has leaned heavily on the metaphor of prophecy to make its foundational theological claim, that Jesus of Nazareth was the Jews' long-awaited Messiah and God's Son. Christian interpreters since New Testament times have argued that the Hebrew Scriptures point in myriad veiled ways to the identity and mission of Jesus as the Christ.

Even our secular society remains interested in the idea of prophecy. Culture analysts have taken up the idea of "prophet" to describe anyone who seems able to predict trends in fashion, business, art, economics, or other cultural arenas. The notion of "speaking truth to power," a description of the prophetic task grounded in Quaker pacifism and made

popular by Yale University chaplain and antiwar activist William
Sloane Coffin (1924–2006),[1] has become a common expression for pro-
claiming any truth that may be received unhappily by those in authority. The Old Testament prophets stand at the beginning of a venerable
tradition of the challenging prophetic voice. They speak truth—to
power and to the powerless alike.

Prophetic stories and oracles in the Bible offer diverse glimpses of
the roles prophets played and their spiritual and political importance
in the life of ancient Israel. Prophets are mentioned in the Pentateuch
(Genesis, Exodus, Leviticus, Numbers, and Deuteronomy) and in the
historical books of the Bible (Joshua, Judges, Samuel, Kings, and
Chronicles). The three major prophets are Isaiah, Jeremiah, and
Ezekiel, and they are joined by the twelve so-called "minor" prophets
("minor" only because their books are shorter): Hosea, Joel, Amos,
Obadiah, Jonah, Micah, Nahum, Habakkuk, Zephaniah, Haggai,
Zechariah, and Malachi.

We will not consider the book of Daniel at length here. In the
Hebrew Scriptures, Daniel is located with the historical books rather
than in the prophetic corpus, and Daniel is properly classified as apocalyptic literature, rather than as a prophetic book. But the Jewish his-
torian Josephus (ca. BCE 37–ca. 100) considers Daniel a prophet,[2]
and early Christian writers see Daniel as a visionary who prophesies
the coming of Christ. The Gospel of Mark draws on Daniel's mysterious allusion to an "abomination that desolates" (Dan. 9:27; 12:11;
Mark 13:14; Matt. 24:15) to interpret the Romans' desecration of the
Jerusalem Temple as a catalyst for eschatological tribulations.
Daniel's vision of the Son of Man descending on the clouds (Dan.
7:13–14) is used by Mark and Matthew of the end-times when Christ
will come again (Mark 13:26; 14:62; Matt. 24:30; 26:64). And Revelation draws heavily on images from Daniel for its own apocalyptic
symbolism regarding the Son of Man, the divine envoy who reveals
secrets to the seer, the book of life, God's heavenly throne room, and
various horned beasts that must be conquered by God's angelic army.

In the Hebrew Scriptures, we see the prophet as wild man (Elijah)
and as sage court adviser (Nathan), as frenzied ecstatic (Saul) and as
letter-writing political prisoner (Jeremiah), as mute seer of disturbing
visions (Ezekiel) and as singer of luminous hymns to God's holiness

(Isaiah); as compassionate intercessor (Moses) and as unrelenting mediator of divine judgment (most of the prophets). Prophets are intermediaries between God and people. The ancient Hebrew prophets facilitated communication between the divine and profane realms. This might involve anointing a new king for Israel or indicting a sitting monarch for royal malfeasance, pleading with God on behalf of the people, or thundering God's words of judgment to a recalcitrant community. The forms that prophetic intermediation took depended on the social context in which the prophetic gift was exercised and the expectations about prophecy that a particular group in Israel's history may have had. Some biblical prophetic books consist entirely of poetic oracles. Others have fragments of story or a lot of story. For example, there is only one brief story in Amos, but the book of Jeremiah has long, detailed passages about events in the life of Jeremiah; the book of Jonah is, in its entirety, an artfully wrought story. The prophetic books are rich in song and history, in poems and stories. We will approach the prophets using three broad categories: what prophets see, what prophets say, and what prophets do.

What Prophets See

In the Hebrew Scriptures, the prophets hear from God in dreams and visions that have significance for individuals and for entire communities. Sometimes these dreams and visions are called such. Other times, the text simply says that the "word of the LORD came to" the prophet, and then what follows has a strong visual component.

> The word of the LORD came to me, saying, "Jeremiah, what do you see?" And I said, "I see a branch of an almond tree." Then the LORD said to me, "You have seen well, for I am watching over my word to perform it." The word of the LORD came to me a second time, saying, "What do you see?" And I said, "I see a boiling pot, tilted away from the north."
> Then the LORD said to me, "Out of the north disaster shall break out on all the inhabitants of the land." (Jer. 1:11–14)

As I looked, a stormy wind came out of the north: a great cloud with brightness around it and fire flashing forth continually, and in the middle of the fire, something like gleaming amber. In the middle of it was something like four living creatures. This was their appearance: they were of human form. Each had four faces, and each of them had four wings. Their legs were straight, and the soles of their feet were like the sole of a calf's foot; and they sparkled like burnished bronze. (Ezek. 1:4–7)

This is what the Lord GOD showed me: the Lord GOD was calling for a shower of fire, and it devoured the great deep and was eating up the land. (Amos 7:4)

The angel who talked with me came forward and said to me, "Look up and see what this is that is coming out." I said, "What is it?" He said, "This is a basket coming out." And he said, "This is their iniquity in all the land." Then a leaden cover was lifted, and there was a woman sitting in the basket! And he said, "This is Wickedness." So he thrust her back into the basket, and pressed the leaden weight down on its mouth. Then I looked up and saw two women coming forward. The wind was in their wings; they had wings like the wings of a stork, and they lifted up the basket between earth and sky. (Zech. 5:5–9)

Through visions and dreams, prophets see God's purposes—sometimes for Israel or Judah, sometimes for the whole earth—symbolized and enacted before their very eyes.

What Prophets Say

The prophets name the people's sins and threaten grave punishment if the people do not turn from their rebellious ways back to obedience to God.

Like the bad figs that are so bad they cannot be eaten, so I will treat King Zedekiah of Judah, his officials, the remnant of Jerusalem who remain in this land, and those who live in the land of Egypt. I will make them a horror, an evil thing, to all the kingdoms of the earth—a disgrace, a byword, a taunt, and a curse in all the places where I shall drive them. And I will send sword, famine, and pestilence upon them, until they are utterly

destroyed from the land that I gave to them and their ancestors.
(Jer. 24:8–10)

> Can I tolerate wicked scales
>   and a bag of dishonest weights?
> Your wealthy are full of violence;
>   your inhabitants speak lies,
>   with tongues of deceit in their mouths.
> Therefore I have begun to strike you down,
>   making you desolate because of your sins.
>   (Mic. 6:11–13)

Sometimes the prophets use gendered imagery to communicate messages about impurity and faithlessness.

> How the faithful city
>   has become a whore!
> She that was full of justice,
> righteousness lodged in her—
>   but now murderers!
>   (Isa. 1:21)

Oracles such as these may be inspiring to those who want to see social injustice and cultic hypocrisy exposed for what they are. But judgment oracles are alarming even when we agree that sin needs to be named and challenged. These oracles evoke anxiety, not least because God seems so rageful and bent on vengeance. We may wrestle with these oracles theologically, if the God we know and worship is not a God who would purposefully will catastrophic loss, sexual violence, emotional anguish, torture, and death for anyone. Feminist and womanist readers (and others) may choose to reject the misogynist metaphors that inform some prophetic rhetoric in the Hebrew Scriptures. Metaphors are not mere stylistic devices. Our imaginations are shaped by metaphor in profound ways. Metaphors teach us how to think about the world and ourselves: they are powerful signals about values and concepts by means of which cultural systems defend certain understandings of truth, power, and relationship. Prophetic rhetoric that uses women's bodies and women's sexuality as signifiers of sinfulness can be harmful to readers who are women and girls. Such rhetoric may be repugnant to readers who do not choose to picture their relationship with God in terms that reflect ancient Israelite males' desire for coercive control of female bodies and autonomy. Thus reading the prophets means not only listening. We may wrestle—vigorously!—with those parts of the Bible that contradict Christian ethics.

The prophets exhort the people to honor God with worship that comes from the heart, and they urge a profound commitment to social justice.

I hate, I despise your festivals,
　　and I take no delight in your solemn assemblies.
Even though you offer me your burnt offerings and grain offerings,
　　I will not accept them;
and the offerings of well-being of your fatted animals
　　I will not look upon.
Take away from me the noise of your songs;
　　I will not listen to the melody of your harps.
But let justice roll down like waters,
　　and righteousness like an ever-flowing stream.

(Amos 5:21–24)

　　"With what shall I come before the LORD,
　　　　and bow myself before God on high?
　　Shall I come before him with burnt offerings,
　　　　with calves a year old?"
　　. . . . .
　　He has told you, O mortal, what is good;
　　　　and what does the LORD require of you
　　but to do justice, and to love kindness,
　　　　and to walk humbly with your God?

(Mic. 6:6, 8)

Prophetic oracles of judgment are directed not just against Israel and Judah, but against enemy nations as well. These oracles make two chief points: first, that the destruction of Israel's enemies is good news for Israel, and second, that God's dominion extends over the whole earth. Even when enemies succeed in their attacks against Israel, it is only because God has empowered them to do so. Oracles against for-

eign nations often mock the arrogance of enemies who attribute their
military success to their own power rather than to God.

> How the hammer of the whole earth
>   is cut down and broken!
> How Babylon has become
>   a horror among the nations!
> You set a snare for yourself and you were caught, O Babylon,
>   but you did not know it;
> you were discovered and seized,
>   because you challenged the LORD.
>
>   (Jer. 50:23–24)

> Thus says the Lord GOD:
> I am against you,
>   Pharaoh, king of Egypt,
> the great dragon sprawling
>   in the midst of its channels,
> saying, "My Nile is my own;
>   I made it for myself."
> I will put hooks in your jaws,
>   and make the fish of your channels stick to your scales.
>
>   (Ezek. 29:3–4)

These oracles may be theologically problematic for believers who are
pacifists and who affirm that God does not will the destruction of
entire nations. Biblical prophetic rhetoric is often violent, and it is an
urgent task of interpretation to find ways to honor Scripture while
resisting the elements of its witness that are ethically troubling.

Some of the most stirring passages in all of Scripture are those in
which the prophets promise God's blessing to those who seek God.

> They shall come and sing aloud on the height of Zion,
>   and they shall be radiant over the goodness of the LORD,
> over the grain, the wine, and the oil,
>   and over the young of the flock and the herd;
> their life shall become like a watered garden,
>   and they shall never languish again.
>
>   (Jer. 31:12)

> The nations shall see your vindication,
>   and all the kings your glory;
> and you shall be called by a new name
>   that the mouth of the LORD will give.
> You shall be a crown of beauty in the hand of the LORD,
>   and a royal diadem in the hand of your God.
>
>   (Isa. 62:2–3)

What Prophets Do

Different regions and settings within ancient Israel had different ways of articulating the role of the Israelite prophet. The *navi'* (female, *nevi'ah*), translated "prophet" in English, is the classical prophet who utters oracles of judgment and salvation, speaking the words of God to an obstinate, sinful people in the public square or confronting kings with sharp words about royal malfeasance. The *hozeh*, usually translated "visionary" or "seer," has revelatory visions from God and interprets them, although the *hozeh*'s function overlaps that of the *navi'* at times. The *ro'eh*, usually translated "diviner," is one who connects God's purposes to the events of everyday life through divination. And we see occasional mentions of the *'ish ha'elohim*, which literally means "man of God" and is sometimes translated "holy man." The *'ish ha'elohim* is an intermediary who knows God's will and may be a wonder-worker. Prophets relay God's words to leaders or to the people, seek out God's purposes in specific situations, and see symbolic visions of things to come.

Some prophets drew on their own lives as material for theological reflection, and they enacted God's word in a kind of "street theater" for dramatic effect with their audiences. In Hosea 1–3, we see that Hosea's marriage to a prostitute is a sign of God's relationship with sinful Israel. Hosea's children are given symbolic names, Lo-ammi ("Not My People") and Lo-ruhamah ("Not Pitied"). Jeremiah is told not to marry or have children:

> You shall not take a wife, nor shall you have sons or daughters in this place. For thus says the LORD concerning the sons and daughters who are born in this place, and concerning the mothers who bear them and the fathers who beget them in this land:

They shall die of deadly diseases. They shall not be lamented, nor shall they be buried; they shall become like dung on the surface of the ground. (Jer. 16:2–4)

This bleak picture of Jeremiah being bereft of family is meant to dramatize the disaster that is about to fall upon Judah. When Ezekiel's wife dies unexpectedly, Ezekiel is told not to mourn but to remain visibly unmoved before his audience. The message is that the people should prepare to suffer horrendous loss when the Babylonians invade Jerusalem and slaughter many Judeans.

Something else prophets do is to enact signs with their bodies, using everyday objects as props. Isaiah is commanded to walk naked and barefoot for three years to demonstrate that the king of Assyria will "lead away the Egyptians as captives and the Ethiopians as exiles, both the young and the old, naked and barefoot, with buttocks uncovered, to the shame of Egypt" (Isa. 20:2–4). Jeremiah is commanded to bury his loincloth in a rocky place at the Euphrates and return to dig it up many days later; the spoiled loincloth symbolizes the ruined pride of Judah and Jerusalem. Ezekiel eats a scroll ("in my mouth it was as sweet as honey") to symbolize God's word being put in his mouth; he is to be mute and bound with ropes as a prisoner inside his house to symbolize that he may go out and speak to the people only when God wants him to speak (Ezek. 3). Prophets live their connection with God, and so prophets' bodies are an essential tool for conveying the prophetic message.

Women Prophets

Prophets' bodies are, of course, gendered, so a word about gender is in order. Women prophets were known in several ancient Near Eastern cultures, for example in Assyria, Babylon, and Emar. It is likely that women functioned as prophets in ancient Israel on a wider scale than Scripture represents. The prophetic stories in the Bible are almost entirely about male prophets and the male leaders with whom they interact. Every one of the fifteen prophetic books in the Hebrew Scriptures features a male prophet. Traces of women prophets are few and far between in the Hebrew Scriptures, and the mentions of women prophets that we do have are fleeting.[3] Miriam, the sister of Aaron and Moses, is called a prophet (Exod. 15:20). She sings a song of triumph after the Israelites have crossed the Red Sea, and she and Aaron challenge Moses to recognize that the Lord speaks through them as well as him (Num. 12:2), but otherwise, Scripture tells us little about her, leaving us to guess at the spiritual power and vision that she might have shared with her people. The book of Isaiah tells us of an unnamed woman prophet who bears Isaiah's son, Maher-shalal-hash-baz. Among the false prophets excoriated by Ezekiel are women prophets who "prophesy out of their own imagination" (Ezek. 13:17), that is, according to their own agendas and not by the word of God. In Nehemiah 6:14 we have a tantalizing brief reference to a female prophet named Noadiah who intimidated the governor Nehemiah and may have led the prophetic opposition to his authority. There are only two stories of women prophets that can be called full-fledged narratives: the story of Deborah in Judges 4–5 and of Huldah in 2 Kings 22.

Deborah is both prophet and judge. The ancient Israelite judges are not judges in our modern sense of legal experts who preside impartially over cases in a court of law. They are charismatic military leaders who do occasionally adjudicate political issues but are famed more for their exploits in battle. Some judges are portrayed as being of dubious character. The judge most famously represented in Western art and film, Samson, is not only a military hero and a Nazirite—one dedicated to the Lord. He is also vengeful and boorish, a barbarian whose brute desires are masked by only a thin veneer of civilization. Another judge, Jephthah, is the son of a prostitute; a ruthless mercenary, Jephthah makes a foolish vow that results in the tragic sacrifice of his beloved daughter. Deborah is the only female judge in the book of Judges, and she is impressive indeed—picture a combination of Xena, Warrior Princess, and Sandra Day O'Connor from the U.S. Supreme Court. Deborah musters ten thousand Israelite troops to fight their Canaanite oppressors, reassures her whining army commander when he loses heart, and leads the Israelites to victory, assisted by another woman, Jael, who delivers the coup de grâce to the Canaanite military commander in her tent. Deborah's prophetic vision—that the Lord would grant Israel victory in this battle—is a powerful affirmation of the "holy war" ethos that we encounter in Joshua and Judges.

The Song of Deborah in Judges 5 is an enigmatic piece of poetry, one of the oldest poems we have in the Hebrew Scriptures. It reflects a fascinating early period in the culture of ancient Israel.

Huldah is an influential prophet who lives in Jerusalem during the reign of King Josiah (ca. 640–609 BCE). Her authority is beyond question, as she is the one whom Josiah's officials consult in a crisis moment. After they have recovered a lost "book of the Law" in the Temple, something like our book of Deuteronomy, Josiah worries that Judah will be punished for not having obeyed the forgotten regulations. Huldah confirms Josiah's fear, prophesying that the Lord will bring disaster on Judah and Jerusalem because the people have failed to observe the Law. That this story has been preserved in 2 Kings 22 is astonishing, given that the Hebrew Scriptures tend to privilege male leadership and ignore or downplay women's roles in the public sphere. To a woman prophet is attributed the most crucial prophecy of the preexilic period: her words provide support for the Josianic reform of worship practices (see 2 Kings 23), a central part of the program promoted by the Deuteronomistic historians.

The Prophetic Word and Prophetic Conflict

The Hebrew Scriptures present us with two radically different views of the prophetic word. There is a striking difference between the prophetic word in the Deuteronomistic History and the prophetic word in the Latter Prophets (Isaiah, Jeremiah, Ezekiel, and the twelve minor prophets). In Samuel and Kings, the prophetic word is always fulfilled. It is always an efficacious word: prophets predict the future, and God's word inevitably comes to pass. But in the Latter Prophets, the perspective is quite different. The prophets have pleaded with the people for generation after generation to no avail. For these prophets, the prophetic word is not something that is inevitably fulfilled. To the contrary, it is resisted and ignored for generations by those who hear it. Thus we are left with a paradox: Scripture presents the prophetic word as irresistibly powerful, and yet prophecy is an urgent invitation that the people can reject.

Prophesies can be disputed. Prophets advised the royal court about whether to submit to an invading enemy and whether to enter into a particular political alliance. Furthermore, prophets frequently maligned the integrity of political and religious officials, in general terms and, in some cases, specifically by name. So officials and their allies sometimes needed to undermine the legitimacy of a prophet in order to counter the damage that the prophet could do to their political authority. Disputes about true and false prophecy raged in political circles in ancient Israel. One stream of thinking was that true prophecies were most likely going to be about doom; those prophets who prophesied peace (*shalom*) were likely trying to please their audiences rather than speaking a true word from God. Prophets argued with each other, wrestling for the mantle of "true prophet" and disparaging their rivals' messages as false prophecy.

We can see visible concern in Deuteronomy about the problem of how to discern a true prophet. Moses is speaking here:

> Then the LORD replied to me: . . . "I will raise up for them a prophet like you from among their own people. I will put my words in the mouth of the prophet. . . . Anyone who does not heed the words that the prophet shall speak in my name, I myself will hold accountable. But any prophet who speaks in the name of other gods, or who presumes to speak in my name a word that I have not commanded the prophet to speak—that prophet shall die." You may say to yourself, "How can we recognize a word that the LORD has not spoken?" If a prophet speaks in the name of the LORD but the thing does not take place or prove true, it is a word that the LORD has not spoken. The prophet has spoken it presumptuously; do not be frightened by it. (Deut. 18:17–22)

This passage says we can test the prophetic word by waiting to see whether it turns out to be verified by actual events. This is not the handiest of criteria for those who need immediate direction from God, of course, as fulfillment could conceivably take years!

There is a dramatic story about prophetic conflict in Jeremiah 28. The political issue has to do with whether Judeans suffering under the occupation of the invading Babylonians in the mid-590s BCE could expect that Babylon will be overthrown soon or only after a long time. A prophet named Hananiah prophesies that within two years, Judean exiles in Babylon will be repatriated and the looted Temple vessels will be returned to Jerusalem. Jeremiah doesn't agree. Wearing a yoke to symbolize the enduring nature of the Babylonian captivity, Jeremiah flings the accusation of false prophecy at Hananiah. Hananiah breaks the yoke off of Jeremiah's neck—we can be sure that there was a substantial scuffle here—to emphasize that Babylon's power would soon be broken. Jeremiah slinks away for the time being, leaving the reader tense with the unresolved drama of the story. Shortly thereafter, Jeremiah prophesies that because Hananiah has "made this people trust in a lie" (Jer. 28:15), he will be dead within a year. Two months later Hananiah dies, a point meant to vindicate Jeremiah's prophecy as the true word of God.

The Prophet for Us Today

The prophetic voice is claimed by many today who seek to influence the direction of church tradition or social policy. And these folks don't always agree with one another! "Prophecy" can be a call to innovative reform or a call to reclaim a particular view of orthodoxy. One Sunday, the rector of my socially progressive Episcopal church preached about the need for prophetic voices to speak for full inclusion of gays and lesbians in the life of the church. Later, I read a sermon delivered that same morning by the rector of a socially conservative Episcopal church who preached about the need for prophetic voices to name homosexuality as an abomination. Each of these pastors was deeply persuaded of the prophetic truth of his own position. Discerning the true voice of prophecy is never a simple thing.

Here are three points to consider as we begin to explore the diverse and distinctive messages of the biblical prophets.

1. *The prophets are mediators of God's holiness in the world.* Some religious traditions emphasize the sacredness of the material world itself. There is wisdom to be found in practices that invite our attentiveness to the beauty and fragility of creation. But for the Old Testament prophets, the Creator is wholly Other than creation. The prophet's task is to mediate God's holiness to a world that cannot fully understand it and doesn't know how to accommodate it. The prophets position themselves in the liminal space between sacred and profane, living a "threshold" life of faith and inviting us into that life. Prophets see the mundane

for what it is—joyous and beautiful sometimes, but also broken and distorted and driven by the self-interest of those in power. The prophets dare to stand between us and God, pleading for us to the Creator of the universe and sharing with us the wondrous and alarming purposes of the God who is so much greater than we could possibly conceive.

2. *The prophets are idealists.* They will not let us rest content with inadequate understandings of God. They urge us to deeper reflection on obedience, love, and justice. They exhort us to practice what we preach. They insist that our worship arise from an integrated love of God and love of neighbor in our daily lives. As Abraham J. Heschel has said, the prophets are uncompromising in their call for true faith and relentless in their attacks on those who fall short:

> To a person endowed with prophetic sight, everyone else appears blind; to a person whose ear perceives God's voice, everyone else appears deaf. No one is just; no knowing is strong enough, no trust complete enough. The prophet hates the approximate, he shuns the middle of the road. . . . There is nothing to hold to except God. . . . The prophet disdains those for whom God's presence is comfort and security; to him it is a challenge, an incessant demand.[4]

If you need affirmation that it's fine to be "good enough" and that doing a lukewarm job is acceptable, don't look to Jeremiah or Hosea! If you are fond of saying that you are a "work in progress" so it's okay that you make mistakes, you'd better not read Ezekiel! The prophets urge us continually to offer our best work, our truest worship, our most disciplined study of God's ways. Walter Brueggemann rightly says that the prophets are disruptive: they "speak in images and metaphors that aim to disrupt, destabilize, and invite to alternative perceptions of reality."[5] Where we are smug, inattentive, or narcissistic, the prophets will disrupt us. The prophets disrupt the ways in which we justify our heartlessness to each other and our halfheartedness toward God. For the prophets are satisfied only with a deep and complete commitment to knowing God and to serving God's people in the world. The prophets do not bless mediocre efforts and half-serious attempts. Is the prophetic vision daunting? Of course it is. But it is God's gift to our confused and struggling world. Perhaps we may consider prophetic idealism not as a bar that is set impossibly high, but as a passionate call for us to offer ourselves fully to God's service. We have only one life to give to our God, and the prophets want to make sure we know what is at stake in every moment of it.

3. *The prophets are our companions.* The prophets know that God loves us. So the prophets can stand with us in solidarity, encouraging us to rejoice in God's mercy and warning us when we stray from God's ways. A true friend will be honest with you if you are hurting yourself. The prophets were the best friends their communities could possibly have had. The prophets are deeply connected to their people, suffering with them, going into exile with them, and rejoicing with them in God's abundant blessings. When we identify ourselves as belonging to the covenant community, we may claim the heritage of the prophets as our own. And we can rejoice that the prophets accompany us on the spiritual journey.

As we explore the prophets together, consider how to appropriate the prophetic witness in your own life. God has acted in history! This is something the prophets proclaim over and over again. God spoke to real people in ancient Israel and transformed the lives of real communities. The prophets witness to a God whose demands are uncompromising and whose love is world-changing. You may not be worried about an encroaching Babylonian army, as Jeremiah was. But you can learn from Jeremiah's willingness to stand up for the truth at great personal cost, as you ponder how to take a public stand on a social issue that matters. You may not be dismayed by impure worship practices, as Ezekiel was. But you can learn from Ezekiel's courageous defense of God's holiness in our contemporary world as you mull how to resist our culture's fetishizing of wealth, sex, and power.

For many today who embrace the idea of prophetic witness, "prophet" evokes the passionate advocate for justice. We may be inspired by the leader of a grassroots movement for civil rights, or we may admire the spiritual authority of one who preaches on behalf of society's most vulnerable citizens. For those of us less sympathetic to prophecy, "prophet" may bring to mind unsavory characters at the margins of society. We may think of the wild-eyed, disheveled man in the public square who rants at passersby as he brandishes a sign saying, "THE END IS NEAR." Or we may roll our eyes at the uncompromising purist who at every party launches into a jeremiad about society's ills while others smile nervously and edge away. Just so, the prophets in the Hebrew Scriptures may inspire us or make us uncomfortable.

But we need to listen. Every community needs visionaries who can see deeply into the mysteries of the sacred on behalf of all of us. Every community needs prophetic voices to call us back to God, to hold us accountable for our misuses of power, and to urge us to compassion for those in need. The challenge and pathos and unpredictability of life can leave us unsettled about where to look for truth. Even in our moments of joy and peace, we sense that what we trust might not be real, or that it might not last, or that we might have forgotten something important. Here, the Old Testament prophets can help us. They can help us open our hearts to God. In the pages that follow, we will explore the brilliant rhetorical artistry and theological power of the prophets of the Hebrew Scriptures. Listen to their stories, reflect on their visions, and hear their call to us today.

Questions for Discussion

1. How are politics and prophecy related?
2. How can ancient ways of revelation make sense to us today, when most of us don't see visions or hear God speaking directly?
3. How have you experienced the prophetic voice in your own life?

2

The Early Prophets: Balaam, Samuel, Nathan, Elijah, and Elisha

*I*srael's reflections on its early experiences in the land of Canaan show us that prophecy was a dramatically important part of the cultural heritage that shaped Israel as a nascent political entity. In ancient Israel's reflections on the monarchy, prophets play an essential role. They offer checks on and supports for kingly power, serving both as the conscience of the royal court and as key advisers in military strategizing.

In Israelite tradition, Moses became known as the paradigmatic prophet, although he is not the first one in the pages of Scripture to be named a prophet (that honor belongs to Abraham in Gen. 20:7). Moses is distinguished from other prophets by the uniqueness of his intimacy with God (Num. 12:6–8); the authority of the figure of Moses as prophet and lawgiver in biblical tradition cannot be overstated. But other early prophets were influential as well. In this chapter, we will explore the story of Balaam, a Mesopotamian seer who is drawn unwillingly into the drama of Israel's conquest of Canaan. Then we will consider the mighty Samuel and the shrewd Nathan, who prophesy in the royal court. Finally, we will reflect on the cycle of stories about Elijah and Elisha, wonder-workers who prophesy in the northern kingdom during the reigns of several kings of Israel.

Balaam

Ancient Israel's conquest stories describe and attempt to justify theologically the Israelites' invasion of Canaan. The Promised

Land was inhabited by many indigenous ethnic groups. According to the genocidal rhetoric of the Deuteronomists, these were to be exterminated. Any ethical reader will be troubled by the narratives of military savagery that we read in the Pentateuch, Joshua, and Judges. The rules for "holy war" in Deuteronomy 20 are merciless:

> As for the towns of these peoples that the LORD your God is giving you as an inheritance, you must not let anything that breathes remain alive. You shall annihilate them—the Hittites and the Amorites, the Canaanites and the Perizzites, the Hivites and the Jebusites—just as the LORD your God has commanded. (Deut. 20:16–17)

This polity of genocide cannot be affirmed by believers today as the purpose of a loving God. Some years ago I was co-teaching a Bible-study series with a friend, a professor of philosophy who had been formed in the evangelical Episcopal tradition. My friend stunned me by saying, "If the Canaanites were as immoral as the Bible says they were, maybe they deserved to be exterminated." I couldn't believe my ears. Now, I am convinced that believers are called to stay present even to biblical texts that shock us. Faithful readers should seek for fruitful ways to read difficult texts such as Deuteronomy 20 in conversation with our God-given reason and our God-inspired commitment to justice. Indeed, the spiritual process of wrestling with God's Holy Word is one crucial way that we grow up into the full stature of Christ. But to simply accept genocidal rhetoric—even in the Bible—would surely be an abomination to the God who has made all creation and loves every creature in it.

Blessedly, in the Balaam stories (Num. 22–24) we can find resources to contest the genocidal rhetoric of holy war. Israel's conquest traditions include some wonderful tales about a foreign seer named Balaam. Balaam is hired by the king of Moab to curse Israel so that the Moabite army can repel the invaders. Archaeologists have found an eighth-century plaster inscription from Deir 'Alla, Jordan, that speaks of a seer named Balaam. So, historically, it seems likely that there was a famous Balaam who was a seer and that the biblical story is drawing on this. In our story, he manages to get past the obstacle of an angel blocking his way to Moab—the amusing story of Balaam and his talking donkey satirizes Balaam for failing to see what is right in front of him (Num. 22:22–35). Balaam arrives on the scene and tries as hard as he can to curse Israel. This story was meant to be ironically amusing as well as instructive; one way we know is that hyperbole is afoot throughout the story. Balaam busily builds numerous altars—seven altars at each of three elevated sites overlooking the Israelite encampment, for a ludicrous total of twenty-one altars—but his frantic attempts to manipulate the divine are fruitless. Balaam tries to speak curses, but each time he can speak only elaborate oracles of blessing. The hyperbolically blessed Israel is safe from its dreaded enemy—but in the very next moment (Num. 25) Israel almost destroys itself when Israelite men mix sexually with Midianite women (something that the laws of holy war strictly forbid), and God punishes them with a plague that fells twenty-four thousand. The ironic point? The threat of war is irrelevant if Israel does not obey God, because Israel will just destroy itself from within.

Balaam is both honored and condemned in the history of interpretation. This foreign seer is addressed directly by the God of Israel, which is a tremendous honor. By this light, Balaam joins the pantheon of righteous outsiders who correctly perceive the purposes of God, including Abimelech in Genesis 20, Jethro in Exodus 18, and Rahab in Joshua 2. But Balaam is also mocked and disparaged, both in the donkey story (even an animal can perceive the angel, but the vaunted seer Balaam cannot) and in later biblical reflections on his role. In various Old and New Testament passages, Balaam is blamed for trying to curse Israel, for being greedy, and for inciting Israel to engage in idolatry and sexual mixing with foreigners.[1] In postbiblical tradition, some texts praise Balaam as a true prophet, but other texts condemn him as an illegitimate sorcerer who caused Israel to sin. The story of Balaam reminds us that God's purposes may be more complex than we can imagine. This mercenary foreign prophet testifies—reluctantly—to the power of Israel's God. His magical manipulations fail; God can use unexpected means to protect and bless God's beloved people. But the larger irony of the Balaam narrative in its setting in Numbers is that Israel's own faithlessness can undermine even the most extravagant blessing that God might bestow. The overall effect of the story of Balaam is to underline the importance of Torah obedience for God's people. There's a lesson here for those of us who eagerly consult our horoscopes or fetishize our Palm Pilot's organizational powers. The path to blessing is through prayer and obedience to God, not through "magical thinking" or frantic manipulation of things we can control.

Samuel

Samuel is a heroic figure in the annals of Israelite prophecy. Samuel is a visionary to whom God speaks, to be sure. But he is also a mighty judge and savvy political adviser who proves himself indispensable to those in authority during the reigns of Saul and David. Samuel is a skillful manipulator of others, something that the biblical historians may be portraying in a subtly critical light.[2] Samuel is dedicated to the service of the Lord from the moment that he is weaned by his mother, Hannah. Admired by all, Samuel grows "both in stature and in favor with the LORD and with the people" (1 Sam. 2:26) and "all Israel from Dan to Beer-sheba knew that Samuel was a trustworthy prophet of the LORD" (1 Sam. 3:20).

Noteworthy are three dramatic points at which Samuel's prophetic witness shows us how to use power faithfully. First, Samuel's faithfulness and strength of character are contrasted early on with the incompetence and immorality of the Israelite priesthood. The priest sons of Eli are excoriated for greedily taking more than their allotted portion of the offerings brought to the Lord at the Shiloh shrine (1 Sam. 2). They are also criticized for "blaspheming God" (1 Sam. 3:13), and Eli is blamed for permitting his sons' corruption to go unchecked. These stories serve a larger political purpose in authorizing the power claims of a particular priestly group, the Zadokites, over the Elide priests and justifying Saul's slaughter of eighty-five Elide priests later (1 Sam. 22). But here at the beginning of Samuel's story, the prophetic critique of the line of Eli points up the trustworthiness and integrity of Samuel. The message is beautifully—some might say chillingly—clear: no true servant of God can be greedy about personal gain and still please God. The point remains relevant today, when we consider Christian leaders who are indicted for embezzlement, and "prosperity gospel" pastors who live outrageously lavish lifestyles at the expense of their congregations. Faithful leaders are called to humble themselves in service of God and God's people.

A second dramatic point: Samuel's trust in God is contrasted with the stubbornness of the Israelite people in their asking for a king (1 Sam. 8; 12). The people desire power—safety from enemies and a strengthened domestic infrastructure are the underlying political issues. They ask for an earthly king instead of trusting in the sovereignty of God. God is displeased ("they have rejected me from being king over them," 1 Sam. 8:7) and has Samuel warn the people about the oppressive ways of earthly kings. This foreshadows the difficulties that Israel will experience under the monarchy. Many kings of Israel and Judah engaged in economic exploitation, ruthlessly suppressed political dissent, and permitted idolatry as part of their pragmatic polity of alliance-making with foreign nations. The sin of idolatry is cited over and over again in the books of Kings as the reason why God allowed Israel and Judah to be defeated by their enemies. Samuel's insistence on trusting in God rather than in earthly leaders is a powerful signal to God's people then and now. All other means of support can fail; God alone is our Rock and our Redeemer.

Finally, Samuel's loyalty to God's purposes is contrasted with the failure of Saul to honor God's stipulations about holy war (1 Sam. 15). The rules of Israelite holy war required that all booty and plunder— including human captives and animals—be dedicated to the Lord through slaughter. When Saul's army defeats the Amalekites, Saul greedily holds back valuable animals and spares Agag, the Amalekite king. God tells Samuel that Saul has "turned back from following me" (1 Sam. 15:11). When Saul tries to bluff his way through the situation ("I have carried out the command of the LORD"), Samuel calls him on it with a scathing ironic reference to the contraband livestock that also subtly disparages Saul's speech: "What then is this bleating of sheep in my ears, and the lowing of cattle that I hear?" (1 Sam. 15:13–14). The kingdom is torn from Saul and given to David. Through this, the biblical writers demonstrate how high the stakes are in every matter of obedience to God's laws. Whatever we may think of the holy-war framework in which this story is told, we can appreciate the teaching that leadership is about serving God and should never be used to gratify our own desires.

These three stories show us a major tension in the ancient Hebrew cultural imagination between prophetic leadership and the flawed choices of priests, people, and kings. Prophets are crucially important in the Deuteronomistic History, for they confirm that God's purposes have never failed in the history of God's people. Personal integrity, unwavering trust in God, and humble servant leadership are essential for any believer who wants to be deeply aligned with the ways of God in human life.

Nathan

The court prophet Nathan is the guarantor and conscience of the Davidic monarchy. He wields substantial power behind the scenes, as we see when Nathan and Bathsheba scheme to ensure that Solomon becomes the next king rather than David's oldest surviving son, Adonijah (1 Kgs. 1). Nathan's role demonstrates the importance of the prophet in the Israelite cultural imagination, both as mediator of divine blessing and judgment and as political adviser.

The complex material about King David is shaped around two extraordinary literary moments in which Nathan is a central figure. The first moment is when God declares through Nathan that the Davidic throne will endure forever (2 Sam. 7). The second moment involves a poignant story about a ewe lamb; Nathan tells this story to David to entrap the king into confessing a terrible sin (2 Sam. 12:1–15).

Second Samuel 7 is a magnificent speech in which God confirms God's love for Israel and blesses the royal house of David forever. In the view of biblical writers, God cares deeply about political structures. In ancient Near Eastern cultures, kings are considered to be anointed by divine fiat; when kings fail, this is interpreted as the withdrawal of divine favor from the monarch. This view of divinely endorsed rule may seem relevant to those today who believe that nations and leaders are indeed chosen by God for specific divine purposes. Other believers, however, may consider national and international political relationships to be the result of human choices, for good or ill: some political developments should be celebrated (for example, public service on behalf of the poor and international collaboration in relief efforts), and others should be deplored (military expansionism, colonial arrogance, economic exploitation).

However you understand the involvement of God in contemporary politics, Nathan's prophecy about the establishment of the Davidic monarchy is compelling. God says of David's offspring, "I will be a father to him, and he shall be a son to me" (2 Sam. 7:14). This underlines the intimate relationship of God with Solomon, and, it is implied, with each subsequent scion of the Davidic dynasty. The king and his people may experience God's wrath from time to time, but God's steadfast love will never be permanently withdrawn again from the one that God has chosen. Historically, Israel's monarchy in fact came to a decisive end with the defeat of Judah by the Babylonians in 586 BCE. But even this could not derail Israel's trust in the divine promises to David expressed in 2 Samuel 7. Fervent hope for restoration of the Davidic line recurs in exilic and postexilic biblical literature. The prophetic speech of Nathan fueled the messianism that blossomed in the late biblical period and on into intertestamental times. Zechariah, Daniel, and the Dead Sea Scrolls all express hope for a messianic ruler. God's promises to David became a central theological claim within Christian traditions about Jesus of Nazareth, as well. New Testament traditions understand Jesus as one in the lineage of David. Look at the artfully constructed genealogy in the first chapter of Matthew. This might look like a boring list of names, but it actually makes some stunning theological claims about Jesus' kingship, hints that God can work through unexpected and even scandalous means to bring about divine purposes, and foreshadows the inclusion of the Gentiles in the early Christian movement.

Every intimate relationship with God involves accountability, of course. Prophets early and late in Israel's history were crystal clear about that. Nathan's prophetic voice is strong indeed in his indictment of David when David commits adultery with Bathsheba and betrays her husband, Uriah, so that he is killed in battle (2 Sam. 11). Nathan relates the following parable in order to ensnare David: A rich man with abundant flocks needs to entertain a traveler. Selfishly hoarding his own ample herds, he takes a poor man's beloved ewe lamb, a creature cherished "like a daughter," which used to drink from the poor man's cup and sleep in his bosom. The rich man's slaughter of the poor man's lamb is an inexcusable abuse of power. Nathan's storytelling is rich with pathos, and David cries out in indignation that the rich man deserves death for his heartlessness. Nathan's thunderous "You are the man!" lays bare the deeper meaning of the parable regarding what David has done to Uriah. God's condemnation is swift and uncompromising: the child of David's and Bathsheba's adulterous union dies.

Listening to Nathan, we know two things: that God will love and bless the line of David forever, and that even those who are under God's enduring protection must choose rightly or face devastating consequences. In the prophetic vision of the Old Testament, grace and accountability inhabit the same space. Those who are blessed by God may rejoice indeed in God's goodness, but there can never be room for arrogance in the life of the faithful. David is lionized as the charismatic king of Israel's golden age, but he is also excoriated as a ruthless, self-absorbed despot who despises God's word. Where the gaze of the people may be occluded—in this case, either from blind devotion to David or from wholesale condemnation of him—the prophets see it all. Thus the prophets are excellent guides for us into the complexity of the life of faith.

Elijah

The stories about Elijah collected in 1 Kings 17 to 2 Kings 2 make for fascinating reading. Elijah the Tishbite begins his career of prophesying and wonder-working during the reign of King Ahab of Israel (869–850 BCE). This prophet is drawn in the tradition of the wild man, something that is found in various forms in many cultures. Generally, the hirsute and rough-mannered wild man has a deep connection with untamed creatures; he succumbs only reluctantly to the social constraints and hypocrisies of civilization. Elijah journeys through the wilderness for long periods of time, is cared for by ravens (1 Kgs. 17:6), and is described as a wild man by those who see him ("a hairy man, with a leather belt around his waist," 2 Kgs. 1:8, is a signal of Elijah's wildness). In the spirituality of many cultures we see a fascination with the man of God—and occasionally the woman of God—who lives in the wilderness. The Desert Fathers of fourth-century Christianity were monks who lived in remote regions of Palestine, Egypt, and Syria. Believers who sought their counsel were moved by their disciplined holiness, their austere and humble manner of life, and their dramatic stories of spiritual battles with demons. In medieval times, the legends of Francis of Assisi drew on the "wild man" mythology: this beloved saint was often depicted wandering barefoot through the countryside conversing with birds and wild animals. Another example: the early twentieth-century fictional character Tarzan. This feral child grows to become a courageous man whose spiritual connection with nature is represented as more profound than the false lures of civilization. Portraits of the holy "wild man," romantic and fabulous though they are, can teach us about ourselves. Reading about Elijah, we may meditate on the need for spiritual strength in the face of temptations and challenges. We are encouraged to discover what we cherish most, and we are spurred to defend our integrity against the superficial norms and predictable betrayals of human society.

Elijah's principal opponents are King Ahab and his wife, Jezebel, a Sidonian princess who is blamed in the Hebrew Scriptures for idolatry and murderous prosecution of the Lord's prophets. The name "Jezebel" in Western culture has become synonymous with sexual immorality, likely because of the passage in Revelation 2:20–23 that describes one "Jezebel" as a woman who incites others to fornication. The Jezebel who is Elijah's enemy is, instead, a defiant royal figure who doesn't hesitate to use her political power to destroy her enemies. Her husband, Ahab, is described as a sinful king who "did evil in the sight of the LORD more than all who were before him" (1 Kgs. 16:30). Ahab is guilty of worshiping the Canaanite deity Baal, and it is subtly suggested that, under his royal imprimatur, child sacrifice was permitted (1 Kgs. 16:34). Ahab and Jezebel are quite a pair.

But Elijah and his God are more than a match for Ahab and Jezebel. The first story in the Elijah cycle showcases Elijah's ability to work wonders in the heart of Jezebel's home territory, in a city called Zarephath in Sidon.[3] During a drought, Elijah is commissioned by God to go to a widow there and be fed by her. When he meets her and requests water and food, she demurs, saying that she and her son are at the point of starvation themselves and are preparing to die. Elijah prophesies that the God of Israel will miraculously replenish her jar of meal and her jug of oil until God sends rain. So it happens, proving that Israel's God has power even in Baal's territory. Later, the son of the widow falls ill and dies. Demonstrating God's power to bring life out of death, Elijah stretches himself upon the child's body and prays fervently. God heeds the voice of the prophet and revives the child. This marvelous story of the power of the prophetic word finds resonance centuries later in the New Testament story of Jesus raising the son of the widow of Nain (Luke 7:11–17). Wherever we see God's servants the prophets at work, we encounter God's mighty power to heal.

The climactic story of Elijah's strife with Ahab and Jezebel involves a battle over true and false prophecy. To strike at the core of the idolatrous religion supporting the regime of Ahab and Jezebel, Elijah "calls out" the 450 prophets of Baal (1 Kgs. 18). He challenges them to a contest: he will prepare an altar with a bull sacrifice, they will prepare an altar similarly, and whichever deity answers his supplicants' prayers by consuming the sacrifice with fire will be proven to be the true God. When there is no response to the Baal prophets' hours of dancing and supplications, Elijah mocks Baal and his devotees. Then he soaks his own altar with water—an extravagant flourish, given that water is a precious commodity in the time of drought in which this story is set. Elijah prays—and God answers! Fire from heaven miraculously consumes Elijah's drenched sacrifice, proving that nothing is too difficult for the God of Israel. In a troubling postscript that underlines the dramatic political stakes involved, Elijah has the false prophets of Baal executed.

This story is a polemic, a sharply partisan argument, against Baal worship. It is intended to encourage the Israelite audience to trust in the God of Israel and his prophets. The entire point of the story can be summed up in Elijah's sarcastic question to the Israelites before the prophetic contest takes place: "How long will you go limping with two different opinions? If the LORD is God, follow him; but if Baal, then follow him" (1 Kgs. 18:21). Elijah's words remind us of the challenge that Joshua had posed to the Israelites once they had settled in the land of Canaan:

"Now if you are unwilling to serve the LORD, choose this day whom you will serve, whether the gods your ancestors served in the region beyond the River or the gods of the Amorites in whose land you are living; but as for me and my household, we will serve the LORD." (Josh. 24:15)

Back then, Joshua's people had thundered their commitment to God, insisting that they would faithfully serve the Lord who had brought them out of Egypt. In the Elijah story centuries later, the people have become confused, their faith weakened. When Elijah challenges them to choose which deity they will follow, the people stay silent—a marked contrast to the robust acclamation of the Israelites in the time of Joshua. The issue has become urgent: idols and their false prophets must be shown to be ineffectual, even laughable. Life itself is at stake—the drought makes that clear—and the Israelites need to know the God who is the source of their flourishing.

So, too, we need to understand that all good things come from the God who made heaven and earth. Elijah's prophetic voice calls to us through the pages of Scripture, inviting us—with an edge of sarcasm—to choose whom we will serve. Our false gods look different than those of the ancient Israelites, to be sure. In much of North American culture, current idols include addiction to the idea of becoming wealthy and the fetishizing of Hollywood glamour. But these things cannot truly transform lives. They cannot quench our thirst, which is at its deepest level a thirst for God and for compassionate life in community. Elijah's defeat of the prophets of Baal calls us back to the love of the One who spoke through the fire of the burning bush (Exod. 3), who spoke through the fiery tongues as of flame on the disciples' heads at Pentecost (Acts 2), and who continues to speak today in Christ's call to die to self and live for others.

A third story about Elijah is of a very different character than the spectacular tales of wonder-working. In 1 Kings 19, the prophet is hunted by Jezebel. Fleeing into the wilderness, the terrified Elijah reaches Mount Horeb, called Sinai in other ancient traditions, where Moses had received the Law centuries earlier. Elijah takes refuge in a cave, but God commands him to come out so that God may "pass by" him. This is an echo of Moses' hiding in the cleft of a rock while God passed by, just before God wrote the second set of Ten Commandments to replace the set that Moses had broken (Exod. 32–34). But here, there is no giving of the Law. Instead, Elijah witnesses a powerful wind, an earthquake, and a fire, but the Lord is "not in" these—the point being that earlier God had appeared to Moses on Sinai with thunder and earthquake and lightning, but in these latter days the divine is no longer manifest in the old ways.

Then Elijah hears the "sound of sheer silence"—a mysterious Hebrew phrase also translated as "a soft murmuring sound" and the famous "still, small voice" so beloved of spiritual directors. Biblical scholar Marvin Sweeney says that God's power is here captured through a paradoxical "combination of presence and absence,"[4] something that may be helpful to us as we consider how we hear God today. God speaks to Elijah, commissioning him to go anoint new kings in Aram and Israel and a new prophet, Elisha. A new age has dawned, and it means the end of the reigns of Ahab and Jezebel. This story is unusual for its depiction of the vulnerability of the prophet. It invites us to see that only in deep listening to God can we discern our prophetic vocation, overcome our fears, and become equipped to create change in our communities.

Elijah is taken up into heaven by a chariot of fire (2 Kgs. 2:11). Interpreters since ancient days have suggested that Elijah never died and will return to earth. In later books of the Bible, Elijah remains a towering spiritual leader. He is portrayed in the book of Malachi as a messianic figure who will help transform society before the apocalyptic Day of the Lord comes:

> Lo, I will send you the prophet Elijah before the great and terrible day of the LORD comes. He will turn the hearts of parents to their children and the hearts of children to their parents, so that I will not come and strike the land with a curse. (Mal. 4:5–6)

In the intertestamental period, Elijah's power was remembered with awe. "Then Elijah arose, a prophet like fire, and his word burned like a torch. . . . How glorious you were, Elijah, in your wondrous deeds! Whose glory is equal to yours?" (Sir. 48:1, 4). The deuterocanonical book of Sirach, dating to the early second century BCE, underlines the matchless reputation of the prophet Elijah in the Hellenistic era. Elijah appears in the New Testament story of the transfiguration, where Jesus' authority is established through his association with Moses and Elijah in a moment outside of the constraints of historical time. The hope of Elijah's return remains strong in contemporary times. Many observant Jews today leave a place for Elijah at the Seder table during the celebration of Passover. They pour a cup of wine for Elijah and open the door of the home to demonstrate their welcome of the mighty prophet and their enduring hope for the messianic age. Christians can learn a profound lesson from the reverence that Elijah has inspired throughout the centuries. We see in Elijah that the prophetic word is powerful indeed, and it is a vital means of healing for the world.

Elisha

When Elijah ascends to heaven in a chariot of fire, his prophetic mantle is taken up by his disciple Elisha. The testy and unpredictable Elisha does his own wonder-working in a series of signs that underscore his prophetic authority. Elisha makes brackish water potable (2 Kgs. 2:19–22) and a poisonous stew edible (4:38–41). He has bears maul some small boys who are mocking him (2:23–24, a disturbing fable that is meant to show the power of the prophetic word for curse as well as for blessing). He creates a miraculous supply of oil for a debt-ridden widow (4:1–7) and a miraculously enhanced supply of barley loaves and grain for a hungry crowd (4:42–44, a story that anticipates Jesus' feeding of the five thousand and the four thousand in the Gospels). Elisha raises a woman's son from the dead (4:18–37) and makes an iron ax head float (6:1–7). He also strikes hostile Aramean troops with blindness, leads them to Samaria, and then heals their blindness so that they can see where they are—deep in enemy territory and at the mercy of the king of Israel, who must be restrained from killing them. This story, likely hilarious to ancient audiences, suggests a playfulness about the power of the prophetic word as well as the more serious point that God works through the prophets to defeat Israel's enemies.

Considering the wondrous feats of Elijah and Elisha can help us see what was important to ancient Israel when it reflected on its prophetic traditions. Just as American folktales about legendary frontiersman Paul Bunyan reveal this country's fascination with heroic strength, outsized adventure, and political autonomy, so Israel's stories about Elijah and Elisha tell us about that culture's values. The stories of Elijah and Elisha show us a divine word that is active and indescribably powerful in the communal life of Israel. The God of Israel is sovereign over the forces of nature, false deities, and Israel's enemies. In desperate times and unexpected places, the prophetic word makes life possible for the marginalized and changes the course of history. Bereaved mothers rejoice in the compassion of God, and Israel as a nation celebrates the power of God over Baal and over its own kings gone astray.

Our God is known through wondrous healing and through the miracle of resurrection. On this point, the testimony of Elijah and Elisha joins the gospel proclamation of Christians throughout the centuries. In the Scriptures of Israel, the prophetic word is a vital force for political, social, and spiritual transformation. Christians know that this transformation continues today in the one who is God's living Word, Jesus Christ.

Questions for Discussion

1. Is there a place in the contemporary church for prophetic wonder-working?
2. What risks face prophetic leaders who become involved with politics?
3. Where do you hear today's prophetic voices challenging injustice and advocating on behalf of the marginalized?

3

Amos

When people think of the Old Testament prophets, they often think of the prophetic witness for social justice. There is good reason for that impression: although a number of the biblical prophets show little interest in the poor, several of them do insist that there is no way to please God without caring for the marginalized and the oppressed. Biblical prophetic traditions see justice and compassion as foundational to Israel's covenant with God. Legal protections for widows, orphans, sojourners, and the landless abound in the Torah. Those who are callous toward the poor dishonor the covenant that is at the heart of Israelite identity.

Economic disenfranchisement has disastrous consequences for human dignity. Liberation theologian Jon Sobrino insists that when we speak of poverty, we need to realize the depths of suffering that we are talking about. Poverty is not just the absence of material wealth. Sobrino says poverty is "an expression of the denial and oppression of humanness, an expression of the need, the contempt, the voicelessness, and [the] anonymity that millions of human beings have suffered. . . . [E]conomic poverty expresses a deep human, anthropological, and social need: the difficulty of forming a home."[1] On many levels, poverty denies the poor a place in human community. It strikes at the very humanity of the poor, and thus it strikes at the heart of the God in whose image all of us have been made. The prophets' call for social justice, then, may be seen not just as a reminder about Torah stipulations for compassion, but rather as an exhortation to stop ignoring and despising the heart of God.

No prophet has a stronger voice for justice than Amos. Christians have long drawn on Amos in their calls for justice. In his famous "I Have a Dream" speech, Martin Luther King Jr. cried out for racial equity, urging civil rights activists to keep working "until justice rolls down like waters, and righteousness like a mighty stream" (Amos 5:24). Amos is uncompromising in his indictment of those who "trample the head of the poor into the dust of the earth, and push the afflicted out of the way" (2:7) and those who exploit the powerless, "buying the poor for silver and the needy for a pair of sandals" (8:6).

Amos may be the paradigmatic social justice prophet, but he is also a master of rhetoric who uses language and imagery brilliantly to persuade his Israelite audience to love God and neighbor. Amos is a savage ironist, undercutting his audience's smugness by the use of intricate rhetorical traps and unexpected reversals. And Amos is a terrifying prophet of judgment whose uncompromising call to spiritual integrity leaves his audience no place to hide. In our exploration of Amos, we will focus on three points: (1) the way Amos ironizes Israel's ancient traditions to compel his audience not to take God's favor for granted; (2) the way Amos uses ambiguity to force us to think more deeply about the life of faith; and (3) the way Amos employs doxologies (hymns of praise) to bring us to a new place of encounter with the Creator.

Amos the Ironist

Amos is an absolute genius of irony. The prophet employs withering sarcasm and deft use of ironic reversals as surgical instruments to probe beneath our defenses, to force an opening for the word of God in our prideful armor of self-confidence. The most stunning example is Amos's thorough ironizing of the exodus tradition. Many biblical traditions draw on the exodus, the story of God's deliverance of Israel from slavery in Egypt (see Exod. 1–15). Central to Israel's theology is the claim that God saved Israel from oppression. The first of the Ten Commandments is based on the deliverance from Egypt: "I am the LORD your God, who brought you out of the land of Egypt, out of the house of slavery; you shall have no other gods before me" (Exod. 20:2–3; Deut. 5:6–7). God's character as deliverer is the basis of Israel's praise and worship. The Psalms sing of God as divine warrior who fought on behalf of Israel (Ps. 44); God is praised for transplanting Israel from Egypt to Canaan as a botanist tends a rescued vine (Ps. 80).

But the songs of the exodus in Amos are in a darker register, full of dissonances and alarming key changes. Amos does not dwell on God's love for Israel or God's tender care of Israel in the wilderness. Amos recites God's mighty deeds: "I . . . led you forty years in the wilderness. . . . I raised up some of your children to be prophets . . ." (Amos 2:10–11), but then shows how Israel has rebelled ("But you . . . commanded the prophets, saying, 'You shall not prophesy'" 2:12). God's deliverance in the past means that Israel is all the more accountable for its choices: "Hear this word that the LORD has spoken against you, O people of Israel, against the whole family that I brought up out of the land of Egypt: You only have I known of all the families of the earth; therefore I will punish you for all your iniquities" (Amos 3:1–2). Israel's chosenness is the very ground on which God will punish Israel for its sin! Amos is saying that from those to whom much has been given, much will be required (Luke 12:48).

Amos eviscerates the idea that rescue by a divine Shepherd is necessarily a good thing. As if to say, "I'll show you the kind of deliverance you can expect, sinful Israel," Amos thunders, "As the shepherd rescues from the mouth of the lion two legs, or a piece of an ear, so shall the people of Israel who live in Samaria be rescued" (Amos 3:12). Go ahead and be smug about God's deliverance, Amos says—this time, your "deliverance" will be as when a shepherd "rescues" some mutilated body part out of the mouth of the lion. And the image of the lion is not there by chance: for Amos, it is none other than God who is the ravening lion, roaring a divine word of indictment against the people (1:2; 3:8). Amos revisits some of the images of that first exodus— the plague of darkness in broad daylight (8:9; see Exod. 10:21–23), the death of the Egyptian firstborn (Amos 8:10; see Exod. 11:4–12:30)— but this time, the plagues are directed against Israel itself. No escape here. And finally, Amos takes the precious memory of that first exodus itself and says that it is of no account in the larger landscape of history: "Are you not like the Ethiopians to me, O people of Israel? says the LORD. Did I not bring Israel up from the land of Egypt, and the Philistines from Caphtor, and the Arameans from Kir?" (Amos 9:7). Unthinkable: the most cherished memory of Israel's election and deliverance from slavery is made, through Amos's brutal words, into nothing special at all. Israel's exodus from Egypt, so formative for the identity and theology of countless generations of Israelites, is here compared to other exoduses that God has enacted on behalf of Israel's enemies, the despised Philistines and Arameans.

What else does Amos ironize? Any tradition in which his audience could have taken refuge from the scathing prophetic gaze. Amos ironizes Israelite worship, offering a faux call to worship with biting sarcasm: "Come to Bethel—and transgress; to Gilgal—and multiply transgression; bring your sacrifices every morning, . . . for so you love to do, O people of Israel!" (4:4–5). Amos mocks ritual lamentation as a response to disaster, intoning an ironic lament over a "dead" Israel whose doom is in fact still approaching (5:1–3). Amos ironizes his audience's hope for the eschatological Day of the LORD. That day will not be the glorious day of redemption that Israel expects: "Alas for you who desire the day of the LORD! Why do you want the day of the LORD? It is darkness, not light; as if someone fled from a lion, and was met by a bear, or went into the house and rested a hand against the wall, and was bitten by a snake" (5:18–19).

Amos's visions, too, are ironic. He sees a basket of summer fruit (the Hebrew word is *qayitz*), normally a sign of nourishment and abundance, but here used as a pun to signal the terrifying end (*qetz*) of the Israelites, whose corpses will be strewn everywhere. The ironies of Amos are ruthless, leaving Israel nowhere to hide from the prophetic word.

Ambiguity as Entrapment

The book of Amos is completely perplexing at key moments. This is part of Amos's strategy to get the prophetic word deep into the hearts and minds of his audience. An excellent example of ambiguity comes up in the opening oracles against foreign nations in Amos 1–2. Many prophetic books contain oracles promising that God would punish Israel's enemies. This was usually good news for Israel—but Amos does something unexpected with the form. Amos's oracles against the nations all begin with, "For three transgressions of [the nation] and for four, I will not *turn it back*"—more on what that means in a moment—

and Amos goes on to say that because the nation has done a series of bad things (in each case the crimes are specific to that nation), God will send a fire upon that nation and destroy its strongholds. The repeated pattern is lovely (repetition is a hallmark of sophisticated poetic artistry in ancient Near Eastern cultures), and it enhances the momentum of the oracles as they progress. But what exactly is going on here? Amos has the opening phrase in each oracle, where God says, "I will not turn it back," remain ambiguous. Turn *what* back? Your English translation may say something like, "I will not revoke the punishment," but that is the translators' guess at an entirely ambiguous phrase. Perhaps God will not turn back the punishment, or God will not hold back the divine hand, or God will not return the relevant nation from exile. Something terrible is going to happen, but we don't know what. Maybe, the audience thinks, we don't need to figure it out. After all, it's just something God is going to do to our enemies.

But at the end of the oracles against the nations, Amos adds Judah and Israel as the last two "foreign" nations that will be obliterated by God's punishment. The Israelite audience has been cheering the destruction of their enemies as the oracles sweep them along. At the climactic moment, when it's too late to stop the juggernaut of enthusiastic assent, Judah and Israel themselves are indicted! This is brilliant entrapment. Now the ambiguity of "I will not turn it back" becomes devastating. Perhaps God will not revoke the punishment, perhaps God will not return the nation of Israel from exile: whatever it means, it's terrifying and it's coming for *us*.

Another way in which Amos uses ambiguity to entrap his audience is through rhetorical questions. Amos alternately lulls and confuses his audience with deceptively simple rhetorical questions. Each time, as the audience puzzles out the answer, the people realize they are convicting themselves. A series of questions in Amos 3 begins innocuously enough: "Do two walk together unless they have made an appointment?" (Expected answer: No.) What is left unspoken becomes more ambiguous and scarier as the questions progress:

- "Does a lion roar in the forest when it has no prey?" (Uh, no. But why are we talking about lions now? Wait, hasn't Amos called God a "roaring lion"? This is starting to make us nervous.)

- "Is a trumpet blown in a city, and the people are not afraid?" (Well, the warning blast of a sentinel's trumpet does make the people afraid, if it's signaling the advance of enemy troops against the city. . . . Yikes, is some enemy coming?)
- "Does disaster befall a city, unless the LORD has done it?" (This is really starting to get alarming. We're supposed to say *no*, the LORD is always in control of events. But if we agree with what this question is implying, maybe we're assenting to disaster coming on our own city. What are we supposed to say?)
- "The Lord GOD has spoken; who can but prophesy?" (This is a hard one. Are we all supposed to prophesy? We don't all have the gift of prophetic discernment, but maybe we should have been able to see the destruction coming. Oh, remember how Amos criticized us, saying we had told the prophets not to prophesy? Maybe God is blaming us for not understanding our situation. There's no way out. We have to agree that God's word is powerful, but if we agree, we'll indict ourselves for not having seen what was coming and for silencing those who could have told us!)

Looking back with hindsight at that first rhetorical question, we see that the "appointment" between the proverbial "two" becomes terrifying: in the unspoken behind Amos's rhetoric, it is God and the prophet who are walking together, discussing the inevitable doom of Israel.

Other scary ambiguous questions come up in Amos. The prophet has God pose this puzzler: "Did you bring to me sacrifices and offerings the forty years in the wilderness, O house of Israel?" (5:25).[2] The audience by now is desperately anxious: "Should we say 'Yes' because God wanted sacrifice then, or 'No' because we relied on God's grace in the wilderness and did not make sacrifices until the Temple was built? Quick, somebody figure out what the right answer is!" Amos presses on relentlessly: sacrifices in the distant past are beside the point, for now Israel will go off into the wilderness of exile, with only their (impotent) idols to protect them. There is no right answer—you cannot win, with Amos!

He asks sarcastically whether Israel thinks it will survive when other nations have not: "Cross over to Calneh, and see; from there go to Hamath the great; then go down to Gath of the Philistines. Are you better than these kingdoms?" (6:2). Israel wants to answer, "Yes, we are better than those kingdoms," but they cannot—not after the searing indictments that Amos has directed against them. But Israel cannot answer, "No, we are no better than those kingdoms," without assenting to their own destruction. Trapped again! And Amos asks, "Do horses run on rocks? Does one plow the sea with oxen?" The expected answer is, "No, obviously not!" but even as Israel is answering, Amos goes on to say that these impossibilities pale beside the unthinkable way in which Israel has perverted justice and foolishly boasted in its own military strength (6:12–13). Ambiguity is a devastating weapon in this prophet's arsenal.

"Prepare to Meet Your God!"

Israel is brought to its knees by Amos's use of irony and ambiguity. In fact, this is precisely Amos's goal: to humble his audience so that they can be spiritually ready to encounter God. Our third theme has to do with how Amos uses hymns of praise to bring us to this encounter with the Creator—a frightening encounter, to be sure, but essential, because the only way to survive is to acknowledge God's power and bow before it. Amos cries out to a sinful Israel, "Prepare to meet your God, O Israel!" (4:12). Following are three doxologies (4:13; 5:8–9; and 9:5–6). These hymns acknowledge God's praiseworthy attributes and mighty deeds, but these are not simple songs of praise. Their real purpose is to heighten the audience's sense of imminent doom. In the first doxology, God is lauded as "the one who forms the mountains, creates the wind, reveals his thoughts to mortals, makes the morning darkness, and treads on the heights of the earth" (4:13). Impressive. But one of those divine attributes gives us pause. "Reveals his thoughts to mortals" reminds us of "Surely the Lord GOD does nothing without revealing his secret to his servants the prophets," in that ominous series of questions in Amos 3. Perhaps the "thoughts" God reveals to mortals are the divine plans to punish Israel.

A note of doom is sounded more clearly in the second doxology. Here God is one who "calls for the waters of the sea, and pours them out on the surface of the earth, . . . who makes destruction flash out against the strong, so that destruction comes upon the fortress" (5:8–9). This is not just the Creator who made the bunnies and flowers; this is a Creator with awe-inspiring power to destroy. The third doxology is more alarming still: God can touch the earth and make it melt, so that "all who live in it mourn" (9:5). There is no escape from this God. Amos's audience is put in the position of having to acknowledge the incomparable power of a Creator who can destroy them in an instant.

Where can Israel turn? Awaiting us is the most profound irony of all: Israel can turn only to God. Only in God, this divine Lion who roars against a sinful people and who can destroy the entire earth, can Israel find its salvation. Amos drives his people to that recognition in the center of the book of Amos, with a threefold exhortation: "Seek me [God] and live" (5:4), "Seek the LORD and live" (5:6), and "Seek good and not evil, that you may live" (5:14). Israel has been lacerated by Amos's razor-sharp ironies, entrapped by potentially death-dealing ambiguities in the prophetic word, and compelled to praise a God who wields unimaginable power to destroy. Its pride broken, its every refuge laid bare, Israel has no choice but to kneel in repentance before the mighty God of Amos.

We all stand condemned by the uncompromising vision of Amos. If we want to claim Amos's prophetic word as our own, we need to take seriously the way in which God's grace holds us accountable. Truly understanding that God is a God of deliverance means humbling ourselves and having compassion for the poor. Amos's terrifying message of doom is intended to turn the hearts of his audience, so that all might seek God and live. Only when we live that prophetic word of deliverance, in all that we preach and practice, can we dare claim that we are God's people.

Questions for Discussion

1. What is the connection between justice and our understanding of who God is?
2. Is there a place for irony and ambiguity in your faith life?
3. What are the ways in which you seek God?

4

Hosea

*H*osea prophesied during a turbulent political time in the latter part of the eighth century. No fewer than six kings sat on the Israelite throne in the space of fifteen years, and four of them were assassinated. Turbulent times have left us with a troubling prophetic book. Hosea is difficult to read: the original Hebrew text is in places so corrupted from scribal error or so conceptually unclear that it is almost impossible to understand. And Hosea is difficult to stomach: the graphically violent language of this prophet is disturbing. The God of Hosea is enraged and hurt by Israel's faithlessness, and so the prophet's language is full of rage and pain. We hear of a God who is "like maggots" and "rottenness" to the people (Hos. 5:12) and who will maul them like a lion (5:14). God will punish the northern kingdom of Israel by bereaving them "until no one is left" and by making them "lead out [their] children for slaughter" (9:12–13). God will tear at Israel's heart like a ravening leopard, like a bear robbed of her cubs (13:7–8). Infertility, miscarriage, and childlessness will destroy Israel (9:11, 14, 16; 13:13). Children will be "dashed in pieces" and "pregnant women ripped open" (13:16).

This is Scripture?

Yes. It is gut-wrenching Scripture that seeks to convey God's anguish about a beloved who has repeatedly gone astray.

There are very beautiful passages in Hosea as well. The prophet sings of God's heartfelt love for Israel as God's own child (11:1–11), and promises that God will be like dew to a repentant Israel (14:5–8). Hosea gives us Israel as mutilated prey and Israel as flourishing olive tree. What's going on here?

Can extreme violence and tender care coexist coherently in a single prophetic book?

They can. But we have to look below the surface of the text in order to understand what Hosea is doing. Hosea is trying to shock his people into repentance. His terrifying rhetoric of divine rage is meant to break the audience's spirit so that they will give up their idols. We have seen that Amos uses scathing irony to destabilize his audience so that they have no choice but to seek God. Hosea uses violent language toward a similar end: to shatter his audience's misplaced confidence so that they can see anew who God is.

In order to grasp the complex dynamics of Hosea's prophecy, we will look at two themes. First, we will consider the story of the prophet's marriage and its interpretation as a theological analogy (Hos. 1–3). Second, we will look at the geographical place names in Hosea to see how the prophet maps out a "history" of Israel's transgressions in order to convict his audience.

The Prophetic Marriage Metaphor

Hosea is the first biblical prophet to use the metaphor of marriage to describe God's covenantal relationship with Israel. At Sinai, Israel was commanded to have no other god but the God of Israel. Hosea dramatizes this commandment not as a political arrangement between a king and his vassals, as some biblical texts do, but as a relationship of love and trust between God and Israel. The marriage metaphor is taken up later in creative ways by Isaiah, Jeremiah, and Ezekiel. Each prophet's use of the marriage metaphor is compelling—and disturbing—in its own way. But Hosea's use of it is unique, for it is grounded in his own life and, as such, is deeply intimate. Hosea is charged by God to use his own marriage to a prostitute, Gomer, as a dramatic illustration of God's relationship with the people of Israel.

Hosea 1–2 portrays the covenant between God and Israel as a fractured union between an adulterous wife and an enraged husband. "Adultery" symbolizes idolatry. The wife has taken many "lovers"— that is, worshiped other gods, including the Canaanite deity Baal. The infuriated prophet wants to strip her, cast her out, and kill her. He says he will have no pity on her children either, because they are "children

of whoredom" (2:4). Here, a word about Hosea's social context may
be helpful. In Middle Eastern cultures from ancient times to today,
patriarchal social norms dictate that men's honor depends on their
protecting the sexual purity of the females in their family. Women's
bodies and women's sexual decisions are entirely under the control of
their fathers, brothers, and other male kin. According to biblical
anthropologist Ken Stone:

> In ethnographic accounts from various parts of the Mediter-
> ranean and the Middle East, one finds that women's sexuality is
> treated by indigenous men as a resource which, like other lim-
> ited resources, can become the object of conflict. The point
> around which this conflict often coalesces is the chastity of
> women, which male kinsmen are compelled to guard with vig-
> ilance. . . . One of the ways in which men can demonstrate their
> masculinity, at least in theory, is through sexual conquest. Sex-
> ual access to women, guarded ferociously by male kinsmen as
> a good which affects their own prestige, can sometimes be used
> by other men as a means with which to increase their prestige in
> turn. . . . The sexual loyalty of a wife is thus an important deter-
> minant of a man's honor, and an unfaithful wife is particularly
> dreaded by men since her unfaithfulness has allowed another
> man to cast shame on her husband.[1]

The biblical marriage metaphor reflects these social norms. When
Hosea portrays God as a betrayed husband and Israel as an adulterous
wife, he is saying that Israel's idolatry with false gods has shamed the
God of Israel. Even today, vicious assaults and so-called "honor
killings" go on in cultures that empower men to control women's bodies. So too, assault and murder are threatened in Hosea.

The violence of this metaphor presents two serious problems for
readers of Hosea. First, some will think that because this is in Scripture, physical abuse of women and children is being approved by God.
Many of us would find that idea unthinkable. But sadly, a significant
number of interpreters through the centuries have argued that the husband's violence here is perfectly justified. Victims of domestic abuse
have been counseled by pastors to "submit" to their batterers, and
Hosea has been cited as biblical grounds for that misguided counsel.

So the first problem is that some readers do read naively and may draw harmful conclusions about gender and power from this text.[2]

Second, Hosea's violent rhetoric has the potential to deform our understanding of who God is. For metaphors are not mere words, not "just" metaphors—they are culturally powerful means of shaping our imaginations. Theological metaphors teach us how to think about God. When we encounter images of God as a raging husband who wants to shame and kill his unfaithful wife, we are being taught to think of God as one who uses power to humiliate and harm people. Even if we don't take the metaphor literally, we may still learn the idea of divinity as punitive. So here, as with all difficult Scripture texts, we need to engage our God-given sense of ethics as we read.

How can we learn from this marriage metaphor while not accepting its dynamics of abuse and misused power? We can seek the deeper truth of Hosea's witness: that idolatry wounds the heart of God. When we look for security in sources other than God, we are spurning the love and protection of the One who has chosen us as a beloved people. Covenant requires not just obedience but intimacy. We are vulnerable in that intimacy—and so is God. Faith is not only about believing. It is about living in a way that shows that we cherish God and rejoice in God's grace.

The "History" of Israel's Transgressions

In order to rejoice fully in God's grace, we need to understand who we are. That means we need to be honest about our sins. Hosea has an absolutely brilliant way of teaching Israel about its sin. The prophet mentions important place-names throughout his prophecies. Look at all the geographical names that come up in Hosea: the Valley of Jezreel, the Valley of Achor, Gilgal, Beth-aven, Mizpah, Tabor, Shittim, Gibeah, Ramah, Adam, Gilead, Shechem, Baal-peor, Beth-arbel, Bethel, Admah, and Zeboiim. Hosea's prophecies are dense with names, and each name tells a story. Each allusion has political significance in the time of Hosea—kings, priests, and other leaders come in for sharp criticism; some of the places are home to Baal shrines—but each also has a more hidden significance having to do with Israel's past.

Hosea is strategically vague about these place-names. Why? Because he makes his audience work to remember what those places have meant in Israel's history. And the picture that emerges isn't pretty. As Hosea's audience does this cultural "research" on place-names, they find that each place stands for Israel's own transgressions. It's like solving a puzzle in which the answers turn out to be all the misdeeds of your youth! Every place in that list has a story associated with it that involves Israel's unfaithfulness. Each one is about Israel's transgressing boundaries by means of illegitimate desire, and especially desire that involves illicit sex or eating. The result is always death.

Thus a dark subtext runs through Hosea's prophecies. As the audience figures out what the prophet is talking about, they indict themselves for their own history of sin. Take a look at the biblical stories connected with Hosea's place-names:

> *Valley of Jezreel*: See 1 Kings 21 and 2 Kings 9–10. Evil King Ahab wants the vineyard of Naboth the Jezreelite and, frustrated, won't eat until he gets what he wants. Jezebel has Naboth killed so Ahab can seize his vineyard. For this and other sins, Ahab and Jezebel are killed by Jehu, who goes in to eat and drink while Jezebel's corpse is being devoured by dogs. Later, Jehu has seventy relatives of Ahab and forty-two relatives of King Ahaziah of Judah butchered in cold blood. Hosea 1:4 connects the coup of Jehu with sin and horrific bloodshed.
>
> *Valley of Achor*: See Joshua 7. This is where a Judahite named Achan keeps holy-war plunder for himself—a big mistake. Joshua finds out, and Achan is stoned to death; his family is burned and crushed under a heap of stones. Hosea 2:15 promises that God will make the sinister Valley of Achor into a "door of hope." Those who remember what had happened earlier in that valley will be all the more grateful for this divine mercy.
>
> *Gilgal and Ramah*: See 1 Samuel 15. Gilgal, a significant regional shrine, is the place where Saul's illegitimate desire leads him to keep plunder for himself and spare King Agag of the Amalekites. The kingdom is torn from Saul, and Samuel hews Agag in pieces. As he lifts his sword, Samuel taunts Agag that his mother will be made childless, anticipating a

major theme in Hosea. Once Agag is dismembered, the blood-spattered Samuel returns to Ramah.

Beth-aven: See 1 Samuel 14. This is a pejorative name for Bethel (an important shrine), but it is also the place where Saul's son Jonathan eats some illicit honey and says something that indicates his disregard for the rules of holy war: "How much better if today the troops had eaten freely of the spoil taken from their enemies" (1 Sam. 14:30). For his insolent act of disobedience, Jonathan barely escapes execution.

Mizpah, Gibeah, and Gilead: See Judges 19–21. These three cities are implicated in the horrendous story of the rape and dismemberment of a Levite's concubine. Intertribal warfare ensues, with more bloodshed and sexual violence. The tribe of Benjamin is almost exterminated—by Israelites! Hosea's audience would shudder at this memory.

Tabor: See Judges 4–5. The reference in Hosea 5 is to a war between Israel and Judah in 735–732 BCE, but the ancient subtext has to do with a battle between Israel and a Canaanite chieftain. The Canaanite commander, Sisera, flees to the tent of a woman named Jael, whose husband is allied with the Canaanites. His presence in an unchaperoned woman's tent hints at the threat of rape. Jael murders him as he sleeps, pounding a tent peg through his skull in an ironic reversal of sexual penetration. Jael's treachery against one who expects alliance is evoked by Hosea, who calls Judah treacherous in its conflict with Israel (Hos. 5:10).

Shittim and Baal-peor: See Numbers 25. Yet more illegitimate desire and death. God's wrath comes swiftly when Israel engages in forbidden sexual relations with Moabite women in the time of Moses. An Israelite man and Midianite woman are impaled in flagrante delicto by a spear thrust from the heroic Phinehas, and a plague sent by God kills 24,000 Israelites.

Shechem: See Genesis 34. Most interpreters read the story of Dinah as a story of rape. But one scholar, Lyn M. Bechtel, has suggested that the story has to do with Jacob's choice to permit marrying outside the clan: when Dinah chooses Shechem, her brothers Simeon and Levi overreact by sexually mutilating and butchering the Shechemites.[3] However we read Genesis 34, it is unquestionably another blood-soaked tale of sexual desire perceived as illegitimate.

> *Adam and Beth-arbel*: These two place-names remain obscure
> to historians. But clearly Hosea associates them with faith-
> lessness (Hos. 6:7) and extreme violence (Hos. 10:14).
> *Admah and Zeboiim*: See Genesis 19 and Deuteronomy 29:23.
> These were cities razed in the destruction of Sodom and
> Gomorrah, punished for wickedness in a story that emphasizes
> the threat of sexual violence. In the aftermath of the destruction,
> Lot's daughters manipulate their father into having incestuous
> sex with them. They conceive the progenitors of two of Israel's
> most intractable enemies, the Moabites and the Ammonites.

The history suggested by the place-names in Hosea is a stunning
history of transgression, illegitimate desire, and death. Every time the
audience figures out another reference in Hosea's subtext, they deepen
their own shame. The prophet's rhetoric is instructive but brutal; as
God says, "I have hewn them by the prophets, I have killed them by
the words of my mouth" (Hos. 6:5). Israel thinks it can rely on itself
and its false gods? Hosea's devastating history lesson teaches them
otherwise. The prophet compels his audience to know their own sinfulness so they will be able to appreciate the gift of love that God has
offered them in the covenant.

God as Nurturer

The book of Hosea is rough going, no question about it. But God does
not only rage and threaten in Hosea. God also murmurs words of love
and healing. Hosea may be one of the most violent expressions of theology that we have in the Bible, but it is also remarkable for its tenderness.
What God wants is an end to the violence that has ravaged Israel's political landscape and its own sense of identity. Hear these words of promise:

> I will abolish the bow, the sword, and war from the land; and I
> will make you lie down in safety. And I will take you for my
> wife forever; I will take you for my wife in righteousness and in
> justice, in steadfast love, and in mercy. (Hos. 2:18–19)

Naming sin makes renewal possible. God is like a loving mother,
teaching the Israelites to walk and nursing them in the distant past. "I

bent down to them and fed them" (11:4), one of the few maternal images of God we have in the Hebrew Scriptures, is a powerful reversal of Hosea's earlier images of infertility, miscarriage, and murdered children. The people of Israel, orphaned by the raging God who has destroyed their idolatrous "mother" (4:5), are now urged to return to a God in whom "the orphan finds mercy" (14:3).

Hosea's diction of violence finally yields to beautiful botanical imagery. God will be like dew in a parched landscape, like an evergreen cypress whose branches offer shelter to Israel (14:5–8). These images of blossoming and leafy shade are unlike anything this prophet has said before. And new metaphors make possible a new understanding of God. It is in this new theology that Israel will discover its own faithfulness, imaged in the Hebrew as fruit (14:8–9).

Hosea's witness is intimate and incarnational. He calls us to look unflinchingly at our own history of sin, and he says that we wound the very heart of God when we reject God's love. It is a hard lesson. But we must face the truth about ourselves in order to know who God is. When we know ourselves, we can begin to see the depth of God's grace to us. Only then can we love God with all our heart, soul, mind, and strength.

Questions for Discussion

1. Does marriage work as a metaphor for God's relationship with the church today?
2. If Hosea were creating a "history of transgression" for Christians, what dark episodes in the life of the church would he ask us to remember?
3. What are the fruits of faithfulness in your own life?

5

Micah

*M*icah of Moresheth was a powerful prophet in ancient Israel. We know this because Micah is quoted as an authority in Jeremiah 26:18–19, at a dramatic moment when Jeremiah is threatened by an angry mob. Jeremiah is suspected of sedition because he has prophesied that Jerusalem will fall to the Babylonian invaders. In his defense, elders cite Micah as a prophet who foretold the fall of Jerusalem ("Zion shall be plowed as a field; Jerusalem shall become a heap of ruins," Mic. 3:12) not out of seditious motives but to spur King Hezekiah to seek God's help. False prophecy and perceived treason are hotly debated issues in the Jeremiah traditions. For the book of Jeremiah to cite Micah at this key juncture means that Micah's stature must have been extraordinary.

Micah is best known for his call to "do justice," "love kindness," and "walk humbly with . . . God" (Mic. 6:8). This stirring injunction has been set to music, emblazoned on posters, embroidered on pillows, and preached countless times. In order to understand the full force of Micah's famous exhortation, we will consider three themes in his prophecy. First, we will look at Micah's view of authentic leadership in the community of faith. Second, we will explore his vision of peace as the fruit of Scripture study. And third, we will reflect on his prophecy about a messiah coming from Bethlehem, an oracle that is taken up in Christian traditions about Jesus of Nazareth.

Authentic Spiritual Leadership

Micah is thunderous in his condemnation of the ways in which the powerful exploit the weak. Those who enjoy resources and influence in the community of faith should use their power on behalf of justice, as the Torah commands. But instead, Micah sees injustice being actively planned and carried out by the wealthy of his society. They "covet fields, and seize them; houses, and take them away; they oppress householder and house" (2:2); women and children are driven from their homes (2:9). Micah is aghast at the ways in which struggling landowners are forced to forfeit their family inheritances.

Here he may be objecting to a large-scale economic change that took place in the latter part of the eighth century BCE. According to historians of ancient Israel, a subsistence-based farming economy that had allowed local farmers to keep their own surpluses gave way to a trade-based economy that benefited the urban elite. Surplus crops were funneled into export, leaving farmers destitute; foreclosures on the property of the poor became increasingly common.[1] Micah compares this economic exploitation to the actions of a foreign enemy. Unforgivably, the wealthy attack those within their own community: "You strip the robe from the peaceful, from those who pass by trustingly with no thought of war" (2:8).

Political officials, priests, and prophets come in for scathing indictment. With privilege and power comes responsibility: leaders should mediate justice to those under their care! But these leaders devour the people's resources greedily. Micah uses the metaphor of cannibalism to express his outrage: the rich "tear the skin off my people, and the flesh off their bones; . . . eat the flesh of my people, flay their skin off them, break their bones in pieces, and chop them up like meat in a kettle" (3:2–3). The influential leaders of this community are nothing better than mercenaries, Micah snarls. They adjudicate cases, teach, and prophesy for money (3:11), while offering cynical assurances of peace—*shalom*—to a people facing ruin.

We have seen that Amos excoriates his people for telling the prophets not to prophesy (Amos 2:12). Micah, too, offers a blistering critique of leaders who are unwilling to hear the truth:

"Do not preach"—thus *they* preach—
    "one should not preach of such things;
    disgrace will not overtake us." . . .
If someone were to go about uttering empty falsehoods,
    saying, "I will preach to you of wine and strong drink,"
    such a one would be the preacher for this people!
                    (Mic. 2:6, 11, author's emphasis)

Micah has no patience for the narcissistic cocoon in which the wealthy and powerful have wrapped themselves. Not only is their greed self-serving; it will lead to the destruction of his beloved people.

Desperate times call for authentic spiritual guidance. The "rulers of the house of Jacob" and the false prophets have so offended God that God will no longer answer them (3:7). What's needed is prophetic leadership. Micah steps up:

But as for me, I am filled with power,
    with the spirit of the LORD,
    and with justice and might,
to declare to Jacob his transgression
    and to Israel his sin.
                    (Mic. 3:8)

His language here is all about power. Two words in the Hebrew, *koach* and *gevurah* ("power" and "might"), can connote the strength of a warrior. But Micah does not wield power for his own gain. No, Micah is filled with the spirit of the Lord and has given himself humbly to God's purposes. Through this pointed language, he reconfigures what power is about.

The prophet is a model of the leadership that people of faith urgently need. Authentic leaders will be honest about the ways in which our communities fall short. Authentic leaders will listen for God's truth instead of seeking their own self-aggrandizement. God is a God of justice! In order to serve God's people, the authentic spiritual leader must be humble and must have a heart for justice.

Scripture Study Brings Peace

For Micah, justice is at the center of God's plan for peace. How can peace be possible for a nation torn apart by the greed of its leaders and savaged by the aggression of foreign nations? The radical claim of Micah 4:1–4 is that in the eschatological future, peace will come into the world through the study of Torah.[2] In this breathtaking vision, nations will stream to Jerusalem to learn the ways of the God of Israel. "For out of Zion shall go forth instruction" (4:2). "Instruction" here is the word *torah*, which means teaching generally but also the gift of the Law that Israel received on Sinai. All the nations will come on pilgrimage to Zion, eager to learn practices of holiness and justice.

Studying the Scriptures will change the world! The biblical understanding of justice and compassion will enlighten every heart, so that "nation shall not lift up sword against nation, neither shall they learn war any more; but they shall all sit under their own vines and under their own fig trees, and no one shall make them afraid" (4:3–4). Devoted Scripture study will yield peace and security for all peoples, not just for Israel. The image of domestic tranquillity here expressly reverses the earlier injustice of Israel's own leaders' forcing people from their homes.

Micah's prophetic word calls for justice within local communities and peace among enemy nations. The Word of God will transform every relationship and every expression of power, locally and internationally. No one shall be afraid! Micah offers us a wonderful challenge for our own study of Scripture. Each time we open the Bible, we should seek to deepen our understanding of God's justice and God's peace. We should search the Scriptures for the love that casts out fear (1 John 4:18) and teach that love to others. When we encounter God's Word, transformation comes, sure as the dawn.

Bethlehem and the Messiah

Looking to the future, Micah promises that a messianic ruler will bring peace to the ends of the earth. The messiah is to come from the village of Bethlehem, insignificant except that it is where David had been anointed king (1 Sam. 16). The messiah's humble origins are in line with Micah's view of authentic leadership. The messianic leader will be powerful, but his might comes from God: "he shall stand and feed his flock in the strength of the LORD, in the majesty of the name of the LORD his God" (Mic. 5:4). The beautiful vision of worldwide peace in Micah 2 is affirmed here, for the messianic ruler will be "the one of peace" (5:5). The phrase reminds us that Isaiah names the messiah "Prince of Peace" (Isa. 9:6).

Micah's oracle is applied in the New Testament to Jesus, who is born in Bethlehem (Matt. 2:5–6). Through the centuries, Christians have seen Bethlehem as a symbol of the radical humility of the incarnation. That dusty little village has become an icon of the way in which God's salvation in Christ reverses our expectations about power and status. God's power is a paradox, according to earthly standards. Micah knows the truth of this, and Christians recognize it anew in the ministry, death, and resurrection of Jesus.

Cultural reflections on Micah's Bethlehem point in diverse ways to the staggering power of God for transformation. In the dark musings of Irish poet William Butler Yeats (1865–1939) and the lyrical romanticism of Episcopal clergyman Phillips Brooks (1835–93), we see the paradox of divine transformation explored through the symbol of Bethlehem. Yeats's apocalyptic poem "The Second Coming"[3] suggests that transformation is bad news for those who thrive on bloodshed and moral confusion. The world is in turmoil:

> Things fall apart; the centre cannot hold;
> Mere anarchy is loosed upon the world,
> The blood-dimmed tide is loosed, and everywhere
> The ceremony of innocence is drowned. . . .

But a monumental shift is coming. Just as Jesus' birth changed everything, so the advent of a new epoch will change everything once again:

> The darkness drops again; but now I know
> That twenty centuries of stony sleep
> Were vexed to nightmare by a rocking cradle,
> And what rough beast, its hour come round at last,
> Slouches towards Bethlehem to be born?

For a world shocked by World War I, Yeats's sinister "rough beast" creates a brilliant modern contrast with any sentimental thoughts of the burbling baby Jesus. In the poet's disturbing vision, even Christendom itself will be changed. Christians may wrestle with Yeats's critique—Yeats had rejected Christianity when he wrote the poem. But from the standpoint of faith, we may certainly agree that just as the incarnation confounded human expectations, so God's continuing transformation of the world may not be what we expect. Then and now, God does not play according to earthly rules of power and powerlessness.

Where Yeats uses Bethlehem ironically to suggest bad news for an immoral and confused modern world, Phillips Brooks sings of the quiet surprise of God's salvation in his poem "O Little Town of Bethlehem":

> How silently, how silently,
>   The wondrous gift is given!
> So God imparts to human hearts
>   The blessings of His heaven.
> No ear may hear His coming,
>   But in this world of sin,
> Where meek souls will receive Him, still
>   The dear Christ enters in.

As Micah urges humility, so Brooks invites us into the meekness of faith. It is "meek souls" who truly understand God's ways, for God's power is made perfect in weakness (2 Cor. 12:9). To follow Christ, we must decline to grasp power for ourselves, just as Jesus did not grasp power but submitted to God's will (Phil. 2:5–8).

"What Does the LORD Require?"

Three insights have emerged from our reading of Micah. First, leaders need to be honest, prophetic, and committed to justice. Second, communities that study Scripture participate in God's ongoing transformation of the world into a place of peace. Third, welcoming the rule of God means opening our hearts to the paradox of God's power made perfect in our weakness. Now we are better prepared to reflect on the famous exhortation in Micah 6:8.

Micah 6 presents a dialogue among prophet, God, and people by means of a "covenant lawsuit," an ancient form that the biblical prophets used to dramatize Israel's indictment for sin. The setting is a metaphorical courtroom where God argues the case for Israel's unfaithfulness. God delivered Israel from slavery in Egypt and gave Israel prophetic and priestly guidance in the persons of Moses, Aaron, and Miriam. God's ironic question, "O my people, what have I done to you? In what have I wearied you?" (6:3), underlines Israel's ingratitude. Micah then creates a "hostile witness" in his courtroom, a worshiper who responds, "With what shall I come before the LORD?" (6:6). This worshiper suggests sarcastically that even "thousands of rams" and "ten thousands of rivers of oil" could not satisfy this God.

The prophet's rebuttal is swift: God's demands are simple and easy to fulfill! "What does the LORD require of you but to do justice, and to love kindness, and to walk humbly with your God?" (6:8). Micah's response draws us back to the Torah—the Scriptures whose truth will bring nothing less than universal peace. We may think here of Deuteronomy 30:14: "The word is very near to you; it is in your mouth and in your heart for you to observe." Justice and kindness and humility are simple things. The true life of faith is within everyone's reach.

But the messianic age is not fully realized yet. In the present, sin and pain continue to harm the people of God. Micah closes with a dynamic dialogue that moves between anguish and prophetic clarity. God and the prophet lament the ways in which the people continue to ignore justice and holiness in their communal life (Mic. 6:9–7:6), and Micah testifies to his trust in God (7:7). Personified Zion responds with her own word of trust despite the present darkness (7:8–10). And finally, Micah pleads with God to save the people, calling on God's compassion and faithfulness (7:14–20).

We live in that place between trust and lament, just as the prophet did. Our broken world cries out for transformation today no less than in the days of Micah. Poverty, racism, war, disease, violence against women and girls, homophobia, political corruption: the challenges facing us are daunting. But Micah shows us a way forward. He urges us to offer prophetic leadership, to engage Scripture faithfully, and to rely on the paradoxical power of God. Do justice, love kindness, and walk humbly with your God! These simple words can empower us for a lifetime of discipleship.

Questions for Discussion

1. What can we learn about Christian leadership from this ancient Hebrew prophet?
2. How might you wield your own power and privilege in a way that is faithful to Micah's witness for justice?
3. If you had to explain the spiritual significance of Bethlehem to someone not of the Christian faith, what would you say?

6

Isaiah

*I*saiah of Jerusalem prophesied during the latter part of the eighth century BCE. Two major military threats disrupted life in Jerusalem during that time: a nasty skirmish called the Syro-Ephraimite War ca. 735–732, and a failed but alarming attack on Jerusalem by the Assyrians in 701. The material we have from Isaiah of Jerusalem, which is located in the first thirty-nine chapters of the book of Isaiah, responds to these two events. But the Isaiah tradition as a whole—the book of Isaiah that you have in your Bible—is a rich and complex literature that spans more than two centuries of prophetic reflection. Later prophets and scribes preserved the eighth-century prophet's words, certainly. But they also reshaped what they had received, and they added new material as God's purposes became clear in subsequent generations.

In Isaiah we find material reflecting not just eighth-century problems, but recovery from the sixth-century Babylonian crisis and reconstruction-era issues after Cyrus of Persia defeated the Babylonians and permitted exiled Judeans to return home in 538 BCE. Scholars call the material from the early postexilic period "Second Isaiah" (chaps. 35 + 40–55); the language and theological perspective of these chapters is markedly different from what we read in earlier chapters of Isaiah. Many expert readers believe that we can discern an even later stage of material, which they dub "Third Isaiah" (chaps. 34 + 56–66). Those chapters have a sharp tone about disputes within the community and a distinctive focus on cultic matters, two characteristics that set them apart from both First and Second Isaiah. There are several other collections of material that may be dated late, including the "Little

Apocalypse of Isaiah" (chaps. 24–27) and political stories about King Hezekiah (chaps. 36–39) that occur also in 2 Kings 18–20. Because different historical situations gave rise to the Isaiah traditions over time, the book of Isaiah is complicated to read. The variation of topics, literary styles, and theological tones makes it hard to read Isaiah straight through as if it were the testimony of a single speaker, and in fact there is no compelling reason to read it that way. The Isaiah traditions give us the gift of diverse witnesses to God's saving work. When we understand the unique perspective of each of those witnesses, we can appreciate better the creative ways in which the prophetic word grows and blossoms in the life of Israel.

The book of Isaiah is rich with intertextual allusions. In a number of places, oracles seem to be responding to other oracles within Isaiah. For just one example, the wonderful vision of the peaceable kingdom that we read in Isaiah 11:6–9, in the context of a prophecy about a messianic figure, is echoed in 65:25 in a new context that has to do with God's creating new heavens and a new earth. Isaiah shows also a knowledge of Exodus traditions and the Psalms. If you had to choose one Old Testament book to have with you for a long sojourn on a desert island, Isaiah would be an excellent choice. Its multilayered testimony to the power of God and its rich allusiveness to other biblical texts make it an extraordinary spiritual resource. This has been recognized by Christians since ancient times. Passages from Isaiah are prominent in lectionaries, especially for Advent and Holy Week. Almost every chapter of Isaiah 40–66 comes up in the Revised Common Lectionary used by many Protestant denominations. Some interpreters have called Isaiah "the fifth Gospel."[1]

Anglican priest and poet George Herbert (1593–1633) wrote a beautiful poem about his longing to grasp the complex truths of Scripture. We might apply his words to Isaiah in particular:

> Oh that I knew how all thy lights combine,
>   And the configurations of their glory!
>   Seeing not only how each verse doth shine,
> But all the constellations of the story.
>
> This verse marks that, and both do make a motion
>   Unto a third, that ten leaves off doth lie:

> Then as dispersèd herbs do watch a potion,
> These three make up some Christian's destiny:
>
> Such are thy secrets, which my life makes good,
>   And comments on thee: for in ev'ry thing
>   Thy words do find me out, and parallels bring,
> And in another make me understood.
>
>   Stars are poor books, and oftentimes do miss:
>   This book of stars lights to eternal bliss.[2]

Herbert rejoiced that Scriptures comment on other Scriptures and respond to them. We may never be able to see the full extent of these inner-biblical dialogues, but it is wonderfully rewarding to try to listen. Encountering dynamic conversations within Scripture, the faithful reader is formed and "found out" by God's Word. We read Isaiah, and Isaiah reads us.

Isaiah of Jerusalem explored theological themes that are elaborated in different ways later in the Isaiah tradition. Robust oracles of judgment in First Isaiah yield to beautiful promises in Second Isaiah. "I dwell in Possibility—/A fairer House than Prose," begins a poem by Emily Dickinson, writing in Amherst, Massachusetts, in the nineteenth century.[3] These poetic words could have been penned by Second Isaiah, who offers luminous visions of restoration. Second Isaiah rhapsodizes about blossoming shrubs and pools of water in the desert, singing that "the lame shall leap like a deer, and the tongue of the speechless sing for joy" (Isa. 35:6). By contrast, the oracles of Third Isaiah are both beautiful and alarming. Third Isaiah envisions a radiant Jerusalem adorned as a bride for God, a wondrous "crown of beauty in the hand of the LORD, and a royal diadem in the hand of your God" (62:3). But Third Isaiah also has a keen sense of the people's sinfulness and a very scary view of God coming in judgment.

One way to approach the book of Isaiah is to track themes as they develop in the Isaiah tradition over time. Here we will consider three thematic trajectories.

1. *Trust in holiness*: First Isaiah's focus on God's holiness illuminates the prophet's mission and prepares us for Second Isaiah's polemic against idols. In Third Isaiah, this motif shows itself as a renewed interest in cultic purity.

2. *God's sovereignty over history*: First Isaiah's insistence that Israel trust in God rather than political alliances is elaborated in Second Isaiah as the motif of God's having planned Israel's political fortunes—for weal and woe—from ancient times. Third Isaiah looks to an eschatological future when God's sovereignty will be shown forth in new heavens and a new earth.

3. *Surviving to serve the world*: First Isaiah's promise of the survival of a purified remnant is dramatized in the Servant Songs of Second Isaiah. The motif of the Suffering Servant (singular) in Second Isaiah then becomes servants (plural), who constitute a renewed and inclusive community in Third Isaiah.

Trust in Holiness

At the beginning of the book, Isaiah tells us who God is: "the Holy One of Israel" (Isa. 1:4). This special divine name, "Holy One of Israel," comes up twenty-five times in the book of Isaiah[4] and only a few times elsewhere in all of Scripture. It represents a theological claim of crucial importance for the Isaiah traditions: God's holiness is powerful. Isaiah of Jerusalem emphasizes that God brings down the proud and holds the sinful accountable—both within God's own people and in foreign nations. This divine judgment proceeds from God's holiness: "The LORD of hosts is exalted by justice, and the Holy God shows himself holy by righteousness" (5:16). Those who do not take God's word seriously are doomed to destruction. Isaiah mocks those sinners who say sarcastically, "Let the plan of the Holy One of Israel hasten to fulfillment, that we may know it!" (5:19). The proud will be devoured by the very holiness they disparage (5:24).

Isaiah is terrified at the magnificence of God's holiness when he receives his commissioning as a prophet, and rightly so—for in Israelite religion, to encounter God's holiness unprepared could get you killed! In the Temple, the prophet sees a vision of the LORD enthroned in glory and attended by six-winged seraphim who sing, "Holy, holy, holy is the LORD of hosts; the whole earth is full of his glory" (6:3). Isaiah knows his own sinfulness and the sinfulness of his people, so he despairs before God's awe-inspiring holiness. But a seraph flies to him with a burning coal from the altar and purifies his lips, blotting out his sin and equipping him for prophetic speech (6:6–7). Isaiah first speaks a mysterious word of judgment against his people: "Make the mind of this people dull, and stop their ears, and shut their eyes, so that they may not look with their eyes, and listen with their ears, and comprehend with their minds, and turn and be healed" (6:10). These verses are cited in all four Gospels and Acts to explain why Jesus teaches by means of perplexing parables and why the gospel is to be taken to the Gentiles. Christian liturgy has adopted the "Holy, holy, holy" verse as the Sanctus we use at Communion. Christian believers may be more awed—and penitent—as they approach the Communion Table if they are mindful that the Sanctus in Isaiah represents a dramatic contrast between God's holiness and the people's sinfulness.

God's holiness is powerful not only for judgment but also for deliverance. The soaring poetry that has come into Christian worship as the "First Song of Isaiah" (12:1–6) urges the community of faith to shout for joy because the Holy One of Israel is mighty to save. This theme of redemption is developed beautifully in Second Isaiah.

Isaiah of Jerusalem is urgently concerned to combat political pragmatism. He tells three dramatic stories to demonstrate the importance of trusting in God's holiness. In Isaiah 7 we hear of King Ahaz of Judah, who is afraid of a hostile coalition mustering against him in the Syro-Ephraimite War. The prophet's message to the anxious king? "If you do not stand firm in faith, you shall not stand at all" (7:9). Trust God!

God gives Ahaz a sign to confirm the power of faith: "Look, the young woman is with child and shall bear a son, and shall name him Immanuel," and before the child has fully matured the enemies' land will be deserted (7:14–16). This sounds like a promise of victory, but it is immediately followed by an oracle of judgment against Judah: defeat at the hands of the cruel Assyrians (7:17). Thus this "sign" is mysterious and alarming. The name of the child, "Immanuel," means "God is with us." This may be taken as a good thing: the powerful presence of the Holy One of Israel in the midst of God's people guarantees their safety and flourishing. The earliest Christian traditions read Isaiah 7:14 as pointing to the incarnation of God in Jesus Christ,[5] so for Christians, this prophecy has come to be an unparalleled promise of hope. But God's presence with the people can also mean judgment. Amos and Hosea knew that, and Isaiah knows it too.

Another story told by the Isaiah traditions shows Hezekiah trusting God during the Assyrians' siege of Jerusalem in 701 (Isa. 36–39). Read Isaiah 36 if you'd like to have your blood run cold at the brutal taunts of the Assyrian envoy. His speech is an ironic tour de force calculated to terrify the Judeans. It would seem that the inhabitants of Jerusalem are doomed, but when Hezekiah prays to God for help, Jerusalem is miraculously saved from the Assyrians, who are struck down by "the angel of the LORD" overnight (37:36).

The third story about trusting in God unfolds not in the arena of international politics but in the body of Hezekiah. The king, wrestling with a potentially fatal illness, turns to God in prayer and is rewarded with healing and fifteen additional years of life. These three stories, taken together, make it crystal clear that trust in God can save us even from overwhelming threats.

Today, Isaiah invites us to think about whether we put too much stock in the systems of politics that govern our nations. Voting is an important way of working within political systems for change. Many political candidates care about the poor and work hard for the upbuilding of local communities. Grassroots organizing and political advocacy can catalyze transformation in the most blighted of neighborhoods—read Mark R. Gornik's *To Live in Peace: Biblical Faith and the Changing Inner City* or Samuel G. Freedman's *Upon This Rock: The Miracles of a Black Church* for inspirational stories of political and social change in Baltimore and East New York.[6] But Isaiah urges us not to rely in any ultimate way on human beings, who can deceive us and fail us. As we work for the transformation of our communities into places of justice and peace, we should remember to pray to the Holy One in whose hand are all the nations of the world, including our own.

Isaiah uses God's holiness to underline the truth of the God of Israel over against false gods. A key result of Israel's punishment ("the glory of Jacob will be brought low," 17:4) will be that "people will regard their Maker, and their eyes will look to the Holy One of Israel; they will not have regard for the [false] altars, the work of their hands, and they will not look to what their own fingers have made" (17:7–8). Idolatry in Isaiah has to do with trusting things that cannot save—which is to say, trusting in false gods, trusting in one's own strength, and trusting in political alliances with other nations. Second Isaiah goes farther, offering a brilliant satire on the futility of idol worship. The poet mocks the benighted person who uses some wood to craft an idol and then builds a fire with the remaining wood to toast his steak sandwich (as it were; see 44:9–20). Idols are powerless statues that need to be carried about and cannot answer those who cry to them (45:20, 46:5–7). How foolish to worship something you made yourself in a spare moment! Second Isaiah's biting sarcasm may make us nervous, if we dare to listen to his deeper point. We might be tempted to think we are not so foolish ourselves—but how often do we implicitly look to our own strength, intellectual creativity, or cultural power to save ourselves? More often than we would like to admit.

Third Isaiah takes up the understanding of God's holiness from earlier voices in the Isaiah tradition, refocusing it on cultic purity. Right worship requires that worshipers be committed to justice and righteousness. Amos had made the point centuries earlier, and Third Isaiah reinforces it, railing against child sacrifice (Isa. 57:5), offerings to idols (57:6–7), funerary cults that permit consultation of the dead (65:3–5), and the failure to keep the kosher laws that guard Israel's identity as a people consecrated to God (66:17).

God's Sovereignty over History

Because we should trust not in political alliances but in God, the Isaiah tradition needs to prove that God is powerful enough to keep believers safe. Demonstrating this is not easy, since Israel and Judah experience horrific military defeats at the hands of several enemies over the course of biblical history. Second Isaiah argues that God has always been in control of human history, even in the dark times when it seemed that Israel's God had been defeated by the gods of Assyria, Egypt, or Babylon. To show God's purposeful and effective presence throughout human history, Second Isaiah lauds God as the incomparable Creator who has planned everything from ancient days: "Have you not known? Have you not heard? Has it not been told you from the beginning? . . . It is he who sits above the circle of the earth, and its inhabitants are like grasshoppers" (Isa. 40:21–22). God may have allowed Israel's enemies to triumph for a time, but now God will do a new thing: God will save Israel by raising up Cyrus of Persia to defeat the Babylonians: "Who has roused a victor from the east, summoned him to his service? . . . Who has performed and done this, calling the generations from the beginning? I, the LORD, am first, and will be with the last" (41:2, 4).

Israel's identity is founded on traditions about God's acts of deliverance long ago. In the time of Second Isaiah, the original exodus under Moses' leadership was ancient history, something that had happened over seven hundred years earlier. Second Isaiah makes a brilliant theological move. He connects the startling new events of his times—the fall of Babylon, Cyrus's edict that exiled Judeans could return home—to what God had planned long ago. Just as God planned all the ancient things that unfolded in Israel's history, so God is now planning a new act of redemption and shares those divine plans in advance: "See, the former things have come to pass, and new things I now declare; before they spring forth, I tell you of them" (42:9). The prophet calls his people to praise God for this new act of deliverance: "Sing to the LORD a new song, his praise from the end of the earth!" (42:10). No other deity is capable of doing what Israel's God has done.

Second Isaiah paints the deliverance of Israel in the sixth century as a new exodus. The poet suggests that God will again make "a way in the sea" (43:16) as in days of old—this time metaphorically, as the escape route back from Babylon does not go through any large bodies of water! God's beloved people will once again journey through the wilderness to the Promised Land (chapter 35).

Third Isaiah continues the motif of God's sovereignty in history by looking to the eschatological future. The material in Isaiah 34 plus chapters 56–66 probably reflects the concerns of a fractious postexilic community seeking how to rebuild its common life after the trauma of displacement and years spent in captivity. Now this culturally decimated people must learn how to interpret the terrors of the past and find a way to live again in hope. Third Isaiah offers a vision of God that connects divine power with the difficult life experience of the Judean people: "For thus says the high and lofty one who inhabits eternity, whose name is Holy: I dwell in the high and holy place, and also with those who are contrite and humble in spirit, to revive the spirit of the humble, and to revive the heart of the contrite" (57:15). The Hebrew words translated "contrite" and "humble in spirit" here could also be translated "crushed" and "abased in spirit"—this is a pastorally brilliant recognition of the spiritual devastation that Judah has suffered. Israel's mighty God is transcendent and eternal, yet God is still present with this humiliated and broken people. A more empowering and healing promise cannot be imagined.

Third Isaiah gives the community renewed agency, inviting them to participate in reconstruction: "You shall be like a watered garden, like a spring of water, whose waters never fail. Your ancient ruins shall be rebuilt; you shall raise up the foundations of many generations; you shall be called the repairer of the breach, the restorer of streets to live in" (58:11–12). And Third Isaiah promises restoration in days to come that will completely eclipse the trauma that Israel has experienced: "Violence shall no more be heard in your land, devastation or destruction within your borders; you shall call your walls Salvation, and your gates Praise" (60:18). The end of human history will be the glorification of Zion. God says, "I am about to create new heavens and a new earth. . . . I am about to create Jerusalem as a joy, and its people as a delight" (65:17–18), and all the earth shall come to worship the God of Israel (66:23).

Surviving to Serve the World

Early and late, the Isaiah traditions reflect on the role of Israel in God's plans. Military conflict and oracles of judgment dominate the material in First Isaiah. Israel is characterized as threatened and vulnerable to the predations of its enemies on the one hand and its wrathful God on the other. Enemy invasions had devastated Zion; the prophet wails, "If the LORD of hosts had not left us a few survivors, we would have been like Sodom, and become like Gomorrah," that is, a smoking ruin (Isa. 1:9; see Gen. 19:28). First Isaiah proposes that a remnant, a small group of survivors, has come through trials and tribulations, "purified" in the process so that they might live with renewed integrity as God's people.

The remnant idea is for the most part alarming, not unlike Amos's vision of "remnant" as a piece of an ear rescued from the mouth of a ravening lion. In Isaiah 6, the prophet's commissioning ends with a vision of wholesale destruction. Isaiah is to speak words of judgment to an uncomprehending people "Until cities lie waste without inhabitant, and houses without people, and the land is utterly desolate" (6:11). Those who remain will be subjected to further purging, God says, as one burns a stump that has remained standing after the tree has been cut down. The last phrase in 6:13, which in Hebrew is a verbless clause linking the elements "seed—holiness—stump," is ambiguous. The sense of it may be judgment: the former holy seed is now merely a stump that will be burned by God's wrath. Or it may be meant as a promise: The formerly burned stump is a holy seed from which new life will spring. In the perspective of Isaiah of Jerusalem, judgment is certainly dominant here. But in the larger witness of the entire book of Isaiah, hope radiates from these words. The ambiguity invites the faith community to repent and, perhaps, to search more deeply in the book of Isaiah for a fuller understanding of God's purposes.

We see ambiguity in another passage about the remnant of Israel, in Isaiah 10:20–23. Reading those four verses, we feel as if we are watching a prophetic argument about what "remnant" should mean theologically. Verse 20 says the remnant will have learned, through its violent experience of purification, to trust in God: "On that day the remnant of Israel and the survivors of the house of Jacob will no more lean on the one who struck them, but will lean on the LORD, the Holy One of Israel, in truth." Excellent! And verse 21 affirms the positive idea of remnant: "A remnant will return, the remnant of Jacob, to the mighty God." But verses 22–23 shoot back, "Look, *only* a remnant will return. Destruction is decreed; retribution comes like a flood!"[7] Here, as in a number of passages in Isaiah, we can see theology being debated before our very eyes.

The aspect of hope represented by the remnant is clearer in Isaiah 11, where green shoots of new life are said to spring from the stem of Jesse (a reference to the Davidic monarchy, David having been Jesse's son). The peaceable kingdom will be inaugurated by God's judgment on the wicked, and "the earth will be full of the knowledge of the LORD as the waters cover the sea" (11:9). Israel would hear in this stirring oracle a promise that their earlier subjugation was over and a life of peace and freedom would be possible.

The purified "remnant" of First Isaiah is developed in later Isaianic tradition in diverse ways that highlight the suffering and eventual triumph of this struggling people. In Second Isaiah we encounter the enigmatic and compelling figure of a servant of God who suffers on behalf of his people and is ultimately vindicated (see Isa. 42:1–4; 49:1–7; 50:4–11; and 52:13–53:12). This Suffering Servant, as he is often called, has a mission to teach Israel and faraway places (the "coastlands"), and he is to bring forth justice in the whole earth. The Servant's faithfulness to God despite adversity allows him to glorify God and serve as a "light to the nations." His suffering and death on behalf of Israel are said to have a mysterious redemptive effect for others. There is nothing like this, theologically speaking, in the rest of the Hebrew Scriptures.

In the cultural setting of ancient Israel, the Servant may represent a prophet (Isaiah himself or perhaps Jeremiah), a righteous king (scholars have suggested Josiah and Cyrus as possibilities), a messianic figure more generally, or the people Israel as a whole. Israel is spoken of as God's "servant" throughout Second Isaiah, but in some of the Servant songs, the Servant is unquestionably being portrayed as an actual individual. It may be the case that the text is purposefully ambiguous—after all, if the Servant were truly a specific individual such as Isaiah or Cyrus, the text could have said so plainly. We may need to hold all of those possibilities in our hearts as we reflect on the profound meaning of the Servant Songs.

Christians embrace an added dimension of theological truth here, for the New Testament interprets the Servant as a prefiguring of Christ (Luke 22:37; Acts 8:26–35). When we have read the entire book of Isaiah and understand just how richly textured the prophecies about the Servant are, we can appreciate that interpretive move by the New Testament writers all the more. We can reflect on ways in which identification with the Servant may highlight Christ's prophetic work for justice, his kingly power, his messianic mission for peace to the ends of the earth, and his incarnational solidarity with the suffering people of Israel. That last possibility, in particular—Christ's solidarity with Israel as God's Servant—has profound implications for our theology and for interfaith relations.

In Third Isaiah we see a shift of focus to all Israelites as God's servants. The community of faith is expanded in startling ways. Eunuchs are invited to worship with confidence among God's people (Isa.

56:4–5), something that goes directly against biblical prohibitions on allowing those with mutilated genitals to enter the congregation (Lev. 21:18–20; Deut. 23:1–3). Foreigners who love the LORD have an honored place on God's holy mountain. The marginalized, including those marginalized by other Scripture texts, will be welcomed into the community of God's faithful people:

> My house shall be called a house of prayer
>   for all peoples.
> Thus says the Lord GOD,
>   who gathers the outcasts of Israel,
> I will gather others to them
>   besides those already gathered.
>   (Isa. 56:7–8)

Remember that Third Isaiah is not all roses. There is a frightening series of "beatitudes" for God's servants that highlights the punishment of those who forsake the LORD:

> My servants shall eat,
>   but you shall be hungry;
> my servants shall drink,
>   but you shall be thirsty;
> my servants shall rejoice,
>   but you shall be put to shame;
> my servants shall sing for gladness of heart,
>   but you shall cry out for pain of heart,
>   and shall wail for anguish of spirit.
>   (65:13–14)

Third Isaiah offers beautiful words of promise to those who heed God's invitation: "The LORD will be your everlasting light, and your God will be your glory" (60:19); "like the days of a tree shall the days of My people be, and my chosen shall long enjoy the work of their hands" (65:22). But God's judgment will be swift and terrible upon those who reject the Holy One of Israel.

In Third Isaiah's inclusive community, we may see very early roots of the Jewish Christian mission to the Gentiles in the first century (Acts 10). We worship a God of love, healing, and inclusion, and it is our joy to proclaim that God to all who have been excluded, harmed, or marginalized. Jesus says, using the words of Third Isaiah, "'The spirit of the Lord GOD is upon me, because the LORD has anointed me; he has sent me to bring good news to the oppressed, to bind up the brokenhearted, to proclaim liberty to the captives, and release to the prisoners'" (Isa. 61:1; see Luke 4:16–21). We who follow Jesus are called to live out these missional words in our own preaching, teaching, and ministry.

Questions for Discussion

1. In what things other than God do you tend to trust?
2. Can you see ways in which God has been sovereign over events in your family's life, or in the life of your community, over generations?
3. How have your own sufferings or experiences of conflict helped you to become a light to others?

7

Jeremiah

The figure of the prophet Jeremiah towers over the landscape of ancient Israel's cultural heritage. Biblical passages outside of the book of Jeremiah mention him by name as a true prophet—a distinctive honor. The author of Chronicles assesses the reign of Zedekiah by noting not just that the king "did . . . evil in the sight of the LORD," an evaluative formula applied to a number of Israel's and Judah's rulers, but that "he did not humble himself before the prophet Jeremiah who spoke from the mouth of the LORD" (2 Chr. 36:12). The authority of Jeremiah is such that kings should bow before him! Other prophets do foretell the fall of Jerusalem and the threat of exile, but only Jeremiah is precise about God's plan for a seventy-year diaspora (Jer. 25:11–12).[1] The prophet's precision impresses later biblical writers, who interpret the exile as fulfillment of the word of Jeremiah (2 Chr. 36:21, 22; Ezra 1:1; Dan. 9:2). Regarding the most horrific event of ancient Israel's history, Jeremiah guided his people and spoke the truth. For this, he is remembered as a prophet of unparalleled spiritual authority.

We can see Jeremiah's influence also in allusions in other biblical books. Benjamin Sommer has explored the ways in which the book of Isaiah uses passages from Jeremiah.[2] Sommer argues that the Suffering Servant is modeled on Jeremiah, that Isaiah confirms Jeremiah's oracles of hope, and that Isaiah reverses Jeremiah's prophecies of doom by using Jeremiah's language in new ways. Here is an example of that last type of interpretive move, with italics showing the shared (Hebrew) language in the two passages.[3]

Jeremiah: "Can a girl *forget* her *ornaments*, or a *bride* her *attire*? Yet my people have *forgotten me*, days without number." (Jer. 2:32)

Isaiah: "But Zion said, 'The LORD has forsaken me, my Lord has *forgotten me*.' Can a woman *forget* her nursing child, or show no compassion for the child of her womb? Even these may *forget*, yet I will not *forget you*. . . . You shall put all of them [viz., the returning exiles] on like an *ornament*, and like a *bride* you shall *bind them on*." (Isa 49:14–15, 18)

Jeremiah speaks for a God who has been abandoned by the people and who responds with punishment. Decades later, Second Isaiah uses Jeremiah's diction to speak for a God who promises to heal the people. In working in this way with prior prophetic tradition, Isaiah both acknowledges the power of Jeremiah's words and rearticulates them in a new register of hope.

Jeremiah's witness is important to the New Testament writers. The Gospel of Matthew says that King Herod's slaughter of young children at the time of Jesus' birth fulfills Jeremiah's prophecy about Rachel weeping for her children (Jer. 31:15; Matt. 2:16–18). Jeremiah's preeminence is signaled when he is said to have been suggested by the crowds as a possibility for the identity of the Son of Man (Matt. 16:14). And Judas's betrayal of Jesus for thirty silver pieces is tied to stories in Jeremiah about the prophet's visit to a potter and purchase of land (Matt. 27:3–10; Jer. 18:1–11; 32:6–25). Paul draws on Jeremiah in his discussion in Romans 2 about the law being written on Gentiles' hearts (Jer. 31:31–34) and about faith requiring metaphorical circumcision of the heart (Jer. 9:26). The reference in Romans 9:21–22 to God as potter may be alluding to Jeremiah 18.[4] Jeremiah's prophecy of a new covenant written on the heart is taken up in Hebrews and applied to the redeeming work of Christ (Heb. 10:15–18).

The life of Jeremiah matters for the testimony of the book that bears his name. Numerous experiences of Jeremiah are narrated in the third person; reflections on what he does and what happens to him are central to the book. The ways in which leaders and the people treat

Jeremiah, for good and for ill, are signs of Israel's responses to the prophetic word. Some individuals support Jeremiah, and they are lauded in the book. Members of a particular scribal family, the Shaphanides, aid Jeremiah in various ways. Receiving special commendation are Ebed-melech the eunuch, who advocates for Jeremiah when he's languishing in a muddy cistern, and the prophet's faithful companion, Baruch the scribe. These two allies are assured that they will be saved from death because they have supported Jeremiah (Jer. 39:15–18; 45:1–5).

But Jeremiah has his adversaries as well, including hostile locals in his village of Anathoth (11:21–23), Pashhur the priest (20:1–6), one Shemaiah of Nehelam (29:24–32), and King Jehoiakim (36:20–32). Jeremiah has a nasty confrontation with Pashhur and gives the priest a derisive nickname, "Terror-all-around," as a sign that terror will fall upon Judah at the hands of the invading Babylonians (Jer. 20:1–6). Jeremiah argues with another prophet, Hananiah, over whether the Judeans' exile in Babylon will be short-lived or lengthy (chap. 28). Hananiah seems to best Jeremiah initially, but Jeremiah is vindicated by the sudden death of Hananiah shortly thereafter. Jeremiah has an unpleasant moment with Jehoiakim when the king destroys a scroll of Jeremiah's prophecies in a slow-motion scene of royal arrogance (chap. 36). Jeremiah's scribe Baruch rewrites the scroll and adds additional words to it, dramatizing the indestructible power of God's word.

The Prophetic Vocation

The commissioning of Jeremiah (1:4–10) is regularly featured in Christian ordination services as confirmation that God raises up leaders for specific ministries. Jeremiah has been consecrated to God's service since before he was born. His vocation: to speak whatever God puts in his mouth. This is dangerous work of plucking up and pulling down, destroying and overthrowing, building and planting (1:10). Jeremiah schools the people in theology and history (he and Amos could vie for the title of Scariest Teacher Ever). For many generations, Israel has disregarded the covenant and ignored God's servants the prophets. Their recalcitrance has finally made intercession impossible: God says to Jeremiah, "As for you, do not pray for this people, do not raise a cry or prayer on their behalf, and do not intercede with me, for I will not hear you" (7:16; 11:14).

The prophet is fiercely opposed in his village and in political circles in Jerusalem. He is threatened, beaten, and driven into hiding. Yet the prophet has no choice but to stand with his people and experience their fate. So Jeremiah laments. This prophet sobs and writhes and shudders and rages! He is bitter about the staggering cost of the prophetic vocation to himself personally, and he is inconsolable over the fate awaiting his people.[5] We see more clearly with Jeremiah than with any other prophet the risks of incarnational prophetic witness.

Jeremiah wails for his battered and suffering people: "Is there no balm in Gilead? Is there no physician there? Why then has the health of my poor people not been restored? O that my head were a spring of water, and my eyes a fountain of tears, so that I might weep day and night for the slain of my poor people!" (8:22–9:1). He also wails for himself. Six poignant laments express the depth of the prophet's agony (11:18–23; 12:1–4; 15:10–18; 17:14–18; 18:19–23, and 20:7–18). Jeremiah is assaulted by the experience of speaking God's terrible word to a hostile people: "The word of the LORD has become for me a reproach and derision all day long. If I say, 'I will not mention him, or speak any more in his name,' then within me there is something like a burning fire shut up in my bones; I am weary with holding it in, and I cannot.... Cursed be the day on which I was born!" (20:8–9, 14). That the tormented Jeremiah later becomes a figure for the suffering Christ is not surprising.

Two thousand years later, George Herbert will wrestle with the pain of adoring a punitive God:

Bitter-sweet

Ah my dear angry Lord,
Since thou dost love, yet strike;
Cast down, yet help afford;
Sure I will do the like.

I will complain, yet praise;
I will bewail, approve;
And all my sour-sweet days
I will lament, and love.[6]

Lament responds to the spiritual truth that pain is real in the lives of the faithful. Not to acknowledge suffering is to remain naive—or disingenuous—about the God whom we worship. Walter Brueggemann says that lament is crucial for mature faith, for lament helps us to take initiative with our God rather than wait passively for rescue, and lament helps us keep the question of justice at the forefront of the community's life.[7] For believers today, the lamenting Jeremiah stands as a model of mature service to God and neighbor.

A Fractured Community

The book of Jeremiah is riven by political arguments and clashing theological voices. Its turbulent witness is true to the experience of a bitterly divided exilic community. To honor that witness, we need to attend to the competing positions that have been preserved in the book. The conflicts in the book of Jeremiah represent larger political conflicts engendered by the desperate times in which Jeremiah lives. Who gets to live, and why? These are urgent questions for any culture decimated by military defeat and colonization.

In many passages within Jeremiah, the chance for repentance is said to be long gone. Doom is inevitable; there will be no remnant and no chance for escape! The intercessions of Jeremiah cannot help, and even the people's repentance will not avail: "The LORD said to me: Do not pray for the welfare of this people. Although they fast, I do not hear their cry, and although they offer burnt offering and grain offering, I do not accept them; but by the sword, by famine, and by pestilence I consume them" (Jer. 14:11–12). In a brutal reversal of exodus language, God agrees to "let the people go"—but not to a place of deliverance, as when Moses led the people to Canaan. "Though Moses and Samuel stood before me, yet my heart would not turn toward this people. Send them out of my sight, and let them go! And when they say to you, 'Where shall we go?' you shall say to them: Thus says the LORD: Those destined for pestilence, to pestilence, and those destined for the sword, to the sword; those destined for famine, to famine, and those destined for captivity, to captivity" (15:1–2).

Per these Jeremiah traditions, God's judgment is irreversible and final: "By your own act you shall lose the heritage that I gave you, and

I will make you serve your enemies in a land that you do not know, for in my anger a fire is kindled that shall burn forever" (17:4). But other Jeremiah traditions offer a markedly different perspective: the coming destruction can be averted through repentance (7:5–7; 18:1–11). Even once the fall of Jerusalem has become unavoidable, these prophetic traditions promise that the exile will last only seventy years and that God's judgment will fall more heavily on some Judahites than on others (25:1–14). Central to this material is the political claim that Judah should submit to the Babylonian invaders and pray for the welfare of Babylon (see chaps. 27–29). Those in diaspora in Babylon are the "true" Israel whom God loves and will restore; those who have remained behind in Judah and who fled to Egypt are abhorrent to God and will be obliterated. These texts reveal an extraordinarily bitter political fight going on in Jeremiah's community during the exilic and early postexilic period. The rhetoric is absolutely vicious. Consider the interpretation of Jeremiah's vision of good and bad figs:

> Like these good figs, so I will regard as good the exiles from Judah, whom I have sent away from this place to the land of the Chaldeans. I will set my eyes upon them for good. . . . Like the bad figs that are so bad they cannot be eaten, so will I treat King Zedekiah of Judah, his officials, the remnant of Jerusalem who remain in this land, and those who live in the land of Egypt. I will make them a horror, an evil thing, to all the kingdoms of the earth—a disgrace, a byword, a taunt, and a curse in all the places where I shall drive them. And I will send sword, famine, and pestilence upon them, until they are utterly destroyed from the land that I gave to them and their ancestors. (Jer. 24:4–10)

Similarly, Jeremiah 42–44 launches ferocious invective against those who took refuge in Egypt.

Thus we see two intractably opposed political positions being argued in the book of Jeremiah. One position—perhaps based in the devastated Judah—argues that all the world stands under the full fury of God's judgment. An eleventh-hour political compromise is despicable and cannot save Judah. Especially eloquent on this point is the tale of the idealist Rechabites in Jeremiah 35, who are lauded for staunchly resisting cultural assimilation. The other position—doubtless promoted by leaders of the Babylonian diaspora community—argues that only those who adopt an accommodationist posture toward Babylon will survive and be redeemed by God.[8] Picture the ancient equivalent of a battle of words between the collaborationist Vichy government of France in the Nazi period and the French resistance. The Judahite community in the book of Jeremiah is in desperate straits, and they are at each other's throats in the battle for survival. It is a sad but entirely predictable result of colonialism that indigenous populations under attack can be all but destroyed by internal strife. The oppressor is too strong to be overcome, so the vulnerable victims fight with each other about viable ways to survive. Here in Jeremiah, as in so many situations of cultural imperialism throughout human history, a pragmatic politics of accommodation clashes with idealistic resistance in the conquered community. Judah is rendered incoherent by its own factionalism, while the oppressor goes about consolidating power and plundering available cultural resources.

Hope amid the Ruins

Jeremiah is rightfully known as a prophet of doom. He insists that true prophets since ancient times have spoken words of doom, not words of false peace (Jer. 28:8–9). The book of Jeremiah opens with an alarming vision of the siege of Jerusalem: "Now I am calling all the tribes of the kingdoms of the north, says the LORD; and they shall come and all of them shall set their thrones at the entrance of the gates of Jerusalem" (1:15). The book closes with a terrifying description of the Babylonians' breach in the Jerusalem city wall, slaughter of the sons of Zedekiah and blinding of the king, carrying of hundreds of people into exile, plundering of the Temple, and execution of seventy-four religious and political leaders (chap. 52). Between the siege images bracketing the book, we encounter many harsh oracles of doom. The book of Jeremiah is dark testimony to the sufferings of an anguished prophet and his broken people.

But there are words of hope here as well. Jeremiah's purchase of land at the height of the Babylonian siege is a prophetic sign-act intended to show that the inhabitants of Judah will eventually regain economic autonomy (chap. 32). Scattered oracles of promise leaven the otherwise relentlessly grim tone of this prophetic book (for example, Jer. 3:12–18; 12:15–16; 17:24–26; and 23:5–8). And we find, smuggled into Jeremiah's brutal rhetoric of judgment, the marvelous "Book of Consolation." That is the name given to Jeremiah 30–31, oracles of healing and restoration so beautiful that scholars have questioned whether they could possibly have come from the historical Jeremiah. Whether these lyrical poems are authentic to Jeremiah or have been added by later prophetic voices, they are here now, deep in the heart of judgment territory. And they sing! These oracles sing of a God who will heal the wounds of the people and cause them to rejoice once again. They sing of a God who will gather the exiles and restore even the most vulnerable of God's beloved people: "I am going to bring them from the land of the north, and gather them from the farthest parts of the earth, among them the blind and the lame, those with child and those in labor, together; a great company, they shall return here" (31:8). Those who are weeping for the dead (so many dead!) will be comforted. And never again will the covenant between God and the people be broken. If the sin of Judah had been "written with an iron pen; with a diamond point it is engraved on the tablet of their hearts" (17:1), well, God can inscribe a new covenant on the hearts of God's people.

> I will put my law within them, and I will write it on their hearts; and I will be their God, and they shall be my people. No longer shall they teach one another, or say to each other, "Know the LORD," for they shall all know me, from the least of them to the greatest, says the LORD; for I will forgive their iniquity, and remember their sin no more. (Jer. 31:33–34)

It will no longer be possible to stray from God. Think of it: no more stubborn sinfulness. No more idolatrous misunderstandings of the holy. No more delusions of self-sufficiency. Everyone will know God! Everyone will understand that we and our communities live only through the mercy of God.

The Book of Consolation is an oasis of hope amid the ruins of Jeremiah's Jerusalem. As we continue to read, we are brought back to the grim reality of life on this side of the new covenant. The terrible sounds of battle gradually filter back into our consciousness. Concerning the houses of Jerusalem, God thunders, "The Chaldeans are coming in to fight and to fill them with the dead bodies of those whom I shall strike down in my anger and my wrath, for I have hidden my face from this city because of all their wickedness" (33:5). It is awful to turn from Jeremiah's lyrical promises of hope back to our violent world. But turn we must. We have to face the truth that the covenant is broken, that justice and love for the neighbor do not yet flourish in our world. And so we must get to work.

Questions for Discussion

1. How do you understand your own spiritual vocation?
2. If lament is an essential part of the mature life of faith, consider: what do you lament in today's world and today's church?
3. How might the faithful believer respond to political and theological disputes without demonizing opponents?

8

Ezekiel

*N*o prophetic testimony in the Hebrew Scriptures is as dramatic and disturbing as that of Ezekiel. This priest sees visions that terrify him into speechlessness and paralysis. He performs an extreme kind of "street theater," using his body in alarming and improbable ways to act out God's purposes for Judah. And he hurls sexually graphic, violent invective at his people in order to shock them out of their complacency. A powerful and creative communicator, Ezekiel finds jaw-dropping ways to dramatize Judah's profaning of the covenant. This prophet delivers an urgent, no-holds-barred message: nothing less than the holiness of God is at stake in the faithlessness of Israel and Judah. Ezekiel will do anything he can to make his people understand.

Ezekiel was deported to Babylon with the first wave of captives in 597, and he speaks to us from the diaspora beginning in 593. A member of the Jerusalem elite, he has been wrenched from his professional service at the Temple and endured what could only have been a strenuous and humiliating journey to Babylon. Ezekiel and the other exiles now live in a profane environment, with restricted means of addressing ritual impurity, no way to offer appropriate sacrifices, and serious constraints on the celebration of their traditional festivals and fasts. All that Ezekiel has worked for as a priest has been turned upside down by the Babylonian invasion. He has been shamed and made powerless.

Yet his people continue to need spiritual leadership, and they have agonized questions about how such a disaster could have befallen God's beloved people and God's holy city. Since the chief duty of Israelite priests is to teach the people the ways of

God, the pressure on Ezekiel is enormous. Somehow, in these circumstances of trauma and deprivation, he must continue to teach the community of exiles about God. He must interpret the truth of ancient traditions and the reality of God in the face of catastrophic loss, despair, and perhaps even nihilism in his audience.

It is a daunting task, and the prophet seems to come close to cracking under the strain. Post-traumatic stress may be visible in the intensity of his sign-acts and the ferocity of his oracles. The prophet goes into an obsessive frenzy when he portrays Israel as an adulterous and nymphomaniacal wife; Ezekiel 16 and 23 employ fetishistic imagery of sexualized violence that some interpreters have named as downright pornographic. And Ezekiel hears God commanding him to do some of the scariest playacting that ancient Israel has ever seen (chap. 4). First, he must build a model of Jerusalem on a brick and enact a siege, making "siegeworks" and placing tiny battering rams around his model city in order to symbolize the Babylonians' impending siege of Jerusalem. Then, bound with cords, Ezekiel must lie on his left side for 390 days to represent the punishment of Israel and then lie on his right side for forty more days to represent the punishment of Judah. He is ordered to bake bread for himself on cow's dung (after he has bargained God down from the revolting prospect of human excrement as the fuel). He must eat the bread and drink water according to a strict rationing schedule, as a sign that the inhabitants of Jerusalem will face famine when their city is besieged. The prophet is mute (catatonic?) for lengthy periods.

Some of this seems to border on hallucinatory illness. It is possible that Ezekiel struggles with a dissociative illness or seizure disorder of some kind.[1] But also on display in Ezekiel's oracles are impressive erudition and astonishing creativity.[2] His poems weave together nuanced allegory and sophisticated allusions to other sacred traditions (for example, chapter 19 and 28:12–19). An oracle about the flashing sword of Babylon (21:9–17) is a masterpiece of performance art. Using onomatopoeic guttural sounds for the sharpening of the sword and repeated interjections that imitate the breathless babbling of a terrified victim, Ezekiel evokes the moment of attack so realistically that our blood runs cold. Ezekiel's recital of the exodus story (20:1–44) is scathing: the leitmotif is not how God redeemed Israel from captivity, but how often God could barely hold back from destroying them, starting before they had even left Egypt! Ezekiel is a master of the slow-building sense of dread. His oracles against Tyre (chaps. 27–28) are brilliant for their elaborate faux praise that yields to devastating ironic reversals. For Judah, he paints a bucolic scene of God as loving shepherd (34:1–16). Just as his audience is relaxing into the lovely images of nurture, he turns it into an oracle of judgment against the "fat sheep," that is, those among the "flock" who exploit the powerless. Ezekiel may be troubled, but he is also a genius.

We will encounter the visceral drama of Ezekiel's prophetic witness through two avenues. First we will journey with him in his visions of the divine chariot, the defiled Jerusalem Temple, and the Valley of Dry Bones. Then we will consider what holiness means for Ezekiel's theology.

Four Living Creatures, Darting "like a Flash of Lightning"

At the river Chebar in Babylon, Ezekiel is stunned to see the glory of God revealed to him. Out of the north in "a great cloud with brightness around it and fire flashing forth" come four winged creatures, each with four faces (human, lion, ox, and eagle) and its own wheel rimmed with eyes all around, capable of moving in any direction without turning. (We find out in Ezek. 10:2 that these are cherubim.) The prophet hears a roar "like the sound of mighty waters." He sees a dome of something "in appearance like sapphire" and something seated on a throne that looks like a human being, gleaming with something like amber and resplendent with what looks like fire. Ezekiel is scrupulously careful to use similes here. He knows that what he is seeing cannot be real amber, real fire, and a real human being, but to suggest that he is seeing the very face of God would be presumptuous.

And God speaks to him from the radiant chariot.

God commissions him to speak to Israel. Ezekiel's task is to be a sentinel, to warn his rebellious people about their sins. God gives the prophet a scroll to eat. It is inscribed with words of lamentation and mourning and woe, and yet in his mouth it is "sweet as honey" (3:3). Israel must be told God's word, "whether they hear or refuse to hear" (2:5, 7; 3:11). Then God departs, with a rush of sound from the living wheels turning and the wings of the four magnificent creatures brushing against one another. Ezekiel sits in shocked silence for seven days.

In this vision we are swept into the major theological currents of the book of Ezekiel. We learn of the indescribable holiness of God, and we understand the compulsion of the prophet to preach words of doom to a sinful people. We see that the transcendent God can come right into the midst of Israel's lived existence, even in a ritually polluted foreign land. God is infinitely dangerous and unutterably powerful—yet God desires covenant relationship.

"Creeping Things and Loathsome Animals"

Fourteen months after his first vision of the chariot, the prophet sees the glory of God again. The hand of God lifts Ezekiel by the hair and takes him "in visions of God to Jerusalem" (Ezek. 8:3), to the Temple, where he sees an idolatrous image in the gate of the inner court. He is commanded to widen a hole in the wall, and when he does so, he can see depicted on the sacred walls "all kinds of creeping things, and loathsome animals, and all the idols of the house of Israel" (8:10). Seventy elders of Israel are offering incense there, a vivid illustration of the corruption of the people's leaders.

God responds by summoning six divine executioners, "each with his weapon for slaughter in his hand." God commands another figure to mark (for mercy) every resident of Jerusalem who deplores the "abominations" that are committed in the city. This mysterious mark on the forehead of the righteous has generated a long history of interpretation. Rabbis in ancient times made many suggestions, among them that the mark—the name for which is the last letter of the Hebrew alphabet (*tav*)—indicated that the righteous person had fulfilled the Torah from *aleph* to *tav*, as it were, "from A to Z." Because in the early Hebrew script *tav* looked like an X, a symbol that in Greek (the letter *chi*) came to stand for "Christ," early church fathers proposed that the saving mark was in the shape of Christ's cross.[3]

The righteous having been marked on the forehead, God then dispatches the executioners to cut down everyone else, from the elderly to little children. The prophet's desperate cry, "Will you destroy all who remain of Israel as you pour out your wrath upon Jerusalem?" implies that Ezekiel fears that few or none are worthy of mercy.

Amos ironizes the exodus by comparing it to God's deliverance of the Philistines and the Arameans (Amos 9:7). Jeremiah puts his own stamp on the exodus tradition by having God "let the people go" to pestilence, famine, the sword, and captivity (Jer. 15:1–2). Now, in the most chilling of these reinterpretations of the exodus, God reenacts the dark night on which the angel of death struck down the Egyptian first-born. This time, the divine executioners slaughter men, women, and children, "passing over" few . . . or perhaps none at all. And this time, Jerusalem has become the new Egypt! The true Israel, then, can only be the exiles in Babylon. As God once led the Israelites out of Egypt, so now the divine chariot proceeds eastward, to the east gate of the Temple (Ezek. 11:1) and thence to "the mountain east of the city" (11:23). God's glory has left Zion and moves eastward to Babylon.

This vision responds to political pressure from those remaining in Judah who are disputing the exiles' claim to be connected to the God of Israel. We have seen that the Jeremiah traditions are a battleground for the diaspora community and those who remain in Judah. In Ezekiel we see that same political dispute. The inhabitants of Jerusalem have said, "They have gone far from the LORD; to us this land is given for a possession" (11:15). Ezekiel's rebuttal? "Sorry, but God has actually moved with *us* to Babylon, abandoning you to destruction." The movement of the divine chariot eastward is one way of making the point. Another is that God says in 11:16, "Though I removed them [the exiles] far away among the nations, and though I scattered them among the countries, yet I have been a sanctuary to them for a little while in the countries where they have gone." The phrase "a sanctuary . . . for a little while" might be translated from the Hebrew as "a little sanctuary" or even, by implication, "a portable shrine." This is a truly innovative theological claim: God's presence may be understood even apart from the sacred space of Zion.[4]

"There Was a Noise, a Rattling, and the Bones Came Together"

In Ezekiel's most famous vision, he is set down by the hand of God in a valley full of dry bones. Everywhere he looks, he sees defilement and abandonment. These human remains have lain on the ground for a very long time, unburied and unmourned. He is commanded to prophesy the breath of God's life-giving spirit into the bones. What astounding power is here attributed to the prophetic word! Ezekiel prophesies, and a thunderous rattling fills the valley. Countless bones, heaps and heaps of bones, come together. "I looked"—this is Ezekiel's equivalent of slow-motion horror unfolding, step by step—"and there were sinews on them, and flesh had come upon them, and skin had covered them; but there was no breath in them" (37:8). What does he see? We should banish any thought of glorious resurrection, happy men and women of Judah brought back to life and dancing for joy. For what Ezekiel sees is an entire valley of fully enfleshed corpses. His terror must be unspeakable.

He prophesies again, "and the breath came into them, and they lived, and stood on their feet, a vast multitude." This is not just any random multitude. The Hebrew there, *chayil gadol me'od me'od*, is best translated as "an exceedingly, exceedingly great army." Ezekiel has just prophesied life—bone by bone, inch by gruesome inch—back into the forgotten armies of Israel and Judah, those slain in battle and so long unburied that all hope had been lost in the diaspora community.

God has answered the people's despairing cry, "Our bones are dried up, and our hope is lost; we are cut off completely" (Ezek. 37:11). God has resurrected an impossibly great army. Israel stands on its feet, ready for battle! The slain of Israel have been mustered for an eschatological battle against all the forces that have ever harmed God's people. The foes, Gog and Magog in Ezekiel 38–39, are symbolic. They are mythological hordes from the frightful north, "the archetypal enemy," in the words of Daniel Block.[5] But they are no match for the God of Israel.

The holiness of God is Israel's most powerful weapon against those who would enslave or destroy them. Ezekiel knows this. Israel's priests have always known this. It is why faithful observance of the Torah is a matter of life and death.

The Demands of Holiness

Ezekiel's priestly vocation gives him the spiritual authority to preach something foundational that the people continually fail to understand: God's holiness is everything. The prophet's chief theological theme, in all of its colorful and shocking elaborations, can be distilled to this:

the holiness of God must not be compromised. God acts for the sake of God's holy name (Ezek. 20:9, 14, 22; 36:22; 39:25; 43:7) in order to preserve God's holiness from defilement and insult. Observance of the Torah is the way that Israel affirms the holiness of God and its own holiness as a people conformed to God's will. The ritual practice of holiness is the means by which Israel comes to know who God is.

When people know the LORD, according to Ezekiel, they will understand God's holiness—and recognize their own loathsomeness. Even when God allows for a few survivors, it is not because of divine love or mercy. It is so that the survivors "may tell of all their abominations among the nations where they go" (12:16) and so others will see that God's ruthless punishment of the people was "not without cause" (14:23). Covenantal faithfulness requires that we acknowledge our own sin. The prophet's deepest commitment is to driving that point home. Ezekiel would not even begin to comprehend our self-indulgent slogan, "I'm just a work in progress—God isn't finished with me yet." He'd respond, "Here's a slogan for you: 'God is holy. You're not. If you don't grasp that soon, you're going to die.'"

Everything God does is toward the end that all will know that God is the LORD. The refrain, "Then they/you shall know that I am the LORD," along with a variant, "Then you shall know that I, the LORD, have spoken," comes up many dozens of times in the book of Ezekiel. It is at the heart of his theology.

- Horrendous slaughter will prove that God is the LORD (Ezek. 6:7, 13; 7:4, 9, 27; 11:10; etc.).
- The exile will prove that God is the LORD (12:15).
- God's destruction of false prophets will prove that God is the LORD (13:23).
- God's forgiveness and reestablishment of the covenant will prove that God is the LORD (16:62).
- God's routing of Judah's enemies will prove that God is the LORD (17:21; 25:5, 7, 11, 17; 26:6; 29:6; 30:8; etc.).
- Ezekiel's own muteness and speech will prove that God is the LORD (24:27).
- God's gift of new life to Israel will prove that God is the LORD (37:6, 13, 14).

Two powerful theological claims come to expression in the refrain that God is the LORD. In the ancient Near East, the military defeat of a people was understood to be evidence that the victors' god had humiliated the losers' god. So one point of Ezekiel's refrain is that the God of Israel is indeed the LORD even though it might seem that the Babylonian deity Marduk had defeated God. An equally important point is that God matters for the life of the people. God complains in 9:9, "The land is full of bloodshed and the city full of perversity; for they say, 'The LORD has forsaken the land, and the LORD does not see.'" God's complaint is that this sinful people takes God to be irrelevant to their current circumstances. "Then they shall know that I am the LORD" stakes a powerful counterclaim: God is fully engaged—for good and for ill—in the lives of God's people!

We can understand the prophet's hyperbolically graphic, sexualized language in the context of his concern for God's holiness. Ezekiel sees with a desperate clarity that our sin threatens the holiness of God. In an honor-based patriarchal society, maintenance of social boundaries is essential to the integrity of the community, and women's sexuality is a marker of those boundaries, which are to be zealously guarded by the males. When Ezekiel uses florid images of female promiscuity to describe Israel and Judah (as in chaps. 16 and 23), he is imputing gendered shame to the males in his audience. He uses highly sexualized language to shock these men into realizing that their faithlessness has brought shame to their kinship groups, to their society, and to their God. God's response is one of extreme sexualized violence: Judah will be stripped bare, stoned, and hacked to pieces (16:39–40). The "honor killings" that still happen in the Middle East and Africa are a grim reminder of the tragic consequences of this male-centered, misogynistic view of honor.

We may resist the social norms that underlie Ezekiel's hyperbolic rhetoric of shame. Much about Ezekiel's use of metaphor cries out for vigorous spiritual wrestling on the part of contemporary readers. But we should acknowledge what is at stake for him: he knows that the only path to redemption is in seeing ourselves for the wretchedly sinful creatures that we are. Ezekiel's offensive, shaming invective is meant to catalyze repentance. For in an astonishing moment, his ferocious God whispers, "I have no pleasure in the death of anyone. . . .

Turn, then, and live." (18:32). Moments of hope in Ezekiel are few, but that is one of them. Here is another: Ezekiel reflects on the tradition of the "new covenant" described lyrically in Jeremiah 31. Rather than saying that all the world will know the LORD, Ezekiel's version promotes the political agenda of the diaspora group. When the exiles return to Judah, they will "remove from it all its detestable things and all its abominations," and then God will give them—the returned exiles only—"one heart and a new spirit" (Ezek. 11:18–19). As we might expect, Ezekiel's version is a bit more gruesome than what we read in Jeremiah. Picture open-heart surgery without anesthesia: "I will remove the heart of stone from their flesh and give them a heart of flesh, so that they may follow my statutes and keep my ordinances and obey them" (Ezek. 11:19–20). But for the volatile Ezekiel, this counts as a glorious promise of transformation.

Hope in Ezekiel comes to its fullest expression in his vision of the eschatological Temple (chaps. 40–48). This vision shows, with a priest's loving detail, the crucial significance of the cultic center of Israel's life. Where God's holiness dwells (43:7), God will be the life and the joy of the people forever! We should not mistake this for a universal vision of community along the lines of Isaiah 56. Boundaries are too important to this priest: "Thus says the Lord GOD: No foreigner, uncircumcised in heart and flesh, of all the foreigners who are among the people of Israel, shall enter my sanctuary" (44:9). But it is a stirring vision nonetheless. The river of life will flow across the Temple threshold and out into the world. Living creatures will flourish wherever the river goes, and the land will burst with miraculous fertility. Trees along its banks will offer all kinds of fruits, and their leaves will be for healing (47:12). "Then they shall know that I am the LORD," thunders the God of Ezekiel over and over again. The people will eventually learn that, the prophet promises. For the name of their new city will no longer be "Jerusalem." It will be simply, "The LORD is There" (48:35). Because of Ezekiel's dramatic, shocking, life-giving prophetic word, the people will learn that God is in their midst.

Ezekiel's Temple vision is later taken up by the author of Revelation. The resplendent new Jerusalem will be open to the faithful of all the nations, all "who are written in the Lamb's book of life" (Rev. 21:27). The radiant glory of God will be the light of the city, something foretold by another of Israel's great prophets (Isa. 60:19–20). The river of the water of life, bright as crystal, will flow from the throne of God. The tree of life will be there, its wondrous fruit available to all now that the sin of Adam and Eve has been redeemed through Christ. And the leaves of the tree will be for the healing of the nations—for Israel and for the Gentiles who have, through the grace of Christ, come to know that God is indeed the Lord.

Questions for Discussion

1. Have you experienced God in your own circumstances of exile, whether metaphorical or actual?
2. How do you listen for the sacred word of God in texts that employ metaphors of horrific violence or the sexualized degradation of women?
3. How might a renewed emphasis on God's holiness be instructive for your own faith community?

9

Other Minor Prophets

*T*he oracles of the minor prophets are called, together, the Book of the Twelve. This book has a fascinating literary history, something that scholars still have not entirely figured out. The minor prophets' books were inscribed on a single scroll in antiquity, in part because they are short and scroll parchments were generally made in longer lengths. But there were also historical and theological reasons for collecting their prophetic witnesses together. Readers have noticed thematic and linguistic connections among the Twelve. Repeated terms are shared among books; in some instances, there are notable links between the ending of one book and the beginning of the next book. For example, the refrain that the LORD is "slow to anger" occurs in Jonah 4, Joel 2, and Nahum 1; this is probably not a coincidence. A noticeable number of shared words connect Micah 7 and Nahum 1; Joel quotes Obadiah extensively; Zechariah alludes to Micah. There was likely editing of these prophetic books over time to enhance their coherence as an integrated witness to the purposes of God.

Biblical scholar Marvin A. Sweeney has argued that each book in the Twelve is responding to a crucial issue raised in the preceding book, so the collection as a whole becomes an organic "conversation" about theological issues.[1] For example, Sweeney says that once Hosea has identified the threat that exists against the northern kingdom of Israel, the next book, Joel, steps in to clarify that Jerusalem has always been at risk as well. We see a brief mention of Edom at the end of Amos; the next book, Obadiah, offers an elaborate indictment of Edom. Thus our reading of the Twelve Prophets will be richest when we consider the interrelationships among them, looking to glimpse the outline of a complex larger story while still appreciating the uniqueness of each prophetic voice.

Joel

Joel is a chilling book. Remember the popular notion of the prophet as a disheveled man with a sign saying "THE END IS NEAR"? Joel could be that prophet! Joel sees visions of "portents in the heavens . . . blood and fire and columns of smoke" and he cries out that "the sun shall be turned to darkness, and the moon to blood, before the great and terrible day of the LORD comes" (Joel 2:30–31).

Joel reflects on many traditions from other biblical books. James Crenshaw says that this prophet's "use of specific phrases" from all over the Bible "gives Joel the appearance of a learned commentator."[2] Biblical books to which Joel alludes include Ezekiel, Amos, Nahum, Obadiah, Zephaniah, and the Psalms. This reminds us that the prophets do not simply receive divine "dictation." They are artists who mine the traditions of Israel for sacred words that can be spoken anew in their own historical contexts.

Joel offers us three unforgettable dramatic images. The first is a plague of locusts "like a powerful army drawn up for battle." They devastate the land, charging like implacable warriors before a terrified populace (Joel 2:5–7). "What the swarming locust left, the hopping locust has eaten, and what the hopping locust left, the destroying locust has eaten" (1:4). The prophet wails that "a nation has invaded my land, powerful and innumerable; its teeth are lions' teeth, and it has the fangs of a lioness" (1:6). Who knew there were so many kinds of locusts and that we should be so frightened of them? We see here the intimate connection of rural Israelites with the land that sustains them. Not only did locusts bring the threat of famine in their wake. Without crops for cereal offerings and grain to feed the animals that the Israelites need for animal sacrifice, right worship of God is no longer possible. From a place of spiritual devastation, Joel begs his people to fast and repent from their sins. "Rend your hearts and not your clothing," the prophet cries (2:13). God requires not superficial ritual but true repentance, a point affirmed by Jesus in his parable about the Pharisee and the tax collector (Luke 18:9–14).

Joel's second unforgettable image is of God gathering all the nations into the dreaded Valley of Jehoshaphat. The location of this valley is unknown, but its alarming name, which means "God judges," may be all we need to know. Vengefulness seethes through these oracles. Joel prophesies that Judahites will sell the children of their enemies into slavery. He invites the nations to "beat your plowshares into swords, and your pruning hooks into spears" (Joel 3:10), a sarcastic reversal of the "swords into plowshares" oracle of peace in Isaiah 2 and Micah 4. In the end-times, God will sit as Judge in this terrible valley and hold the nations accountable for what they have done to God's people over the centuries.

Joel's third dramatic image is of God's spirit being poured out upon all flesh. "Your sons and your daughters shall prophesy, your old men shall dream dreams, and your young men shall see visions" (Joel 2:28). All the world will testify to God's truth and power! This marvelous prophecy is used in Acts 2 to interpret the falling of the Holy Spirit upon the apostles at Pentecost. Joel's witness to the power of the Spirit has become a foundational text for Christian charismatic and holiness churches, including Pentecostal groups, some streams of Methodism, and the Church of the Nazarene.

Obadiah

At twenty-one verses long, Obadiah is the shortest book in the Old Testament, but it packs quite a punch with its vicious invective against Edom. The Genesis stories about Jacob and Esau are stories of origin that tell us about the fraternal tensions between Israel (represented by Jacob) and Edom (represented by Esau). When the Babylonians sacked Jerusalem in the sixth century BCE, Edom should have helped its "brother." But, instead, the Edomites did "slaughter and violence . . . to your brother Jacob" (v. 10). Edom gloated over Judah's disaster, looted, and betrayed Judahite fugitives to the Babylonians. And Obadiah is bitter to the core. As William Brown notes, "The rights and obligations of kinship have been flagrantly violated, and the moral outrage of hurt and betrayal runs deep."[3]

Obadiah insists that the God whom Israel worships is a God of justice. Recompense will be meted out to all those who have harmed God's people: "As you have done, it shall be done to you; your deeds shall return on your own head" (v. 15). This kind of biblical literature—oracles against foreign nations, psalms of imprecation, and other expressions of rage against enemies—gives encouragement to a people ravaged by military defeat and exile. It is important for despairing Israelites to hear that the horrors they have experienced will not go unrequited. Essential to Israel's cultural survival has been the claim that God is stronger than any human foe.

Christians must follow Jesus' exhortation to love our enemies rather than seek their destruction (Matt. 5:43–48; Luke 6:27–28). But Obadiah creates a place in our sacred literature where pain and anger can be named, and that is valuable. Without honesty about our rage at the horrors enacted in human history, our faith is in danger of becoming sentimental and irrelevant. So even though our theology should not be determined in any simplistic way by Obadiah's perspective, we must listen. For in listening, we can honor the pain of his people.

Jonah

The story of Jonah is a marvel of literary artistry. It was written late in the biblical period, so the author knew of the fall of the northern kingdom of Israel to Assyria in 721 BCE, the fall of Nineveh to an army of Medes and Babylonians in 612, and the fall of Jerusalem to the Babylonians in 586. The book of Jonah skillfully weaves together a nuanced characterization of the reluctant prophet and a plot steeped in dramatic irony and suspense.

The world of Jonah is topsy-turvy: nothing is what it should be, and there are surprises around every corner. Jonah combines elements of fable and satire in order to ironize virtually everything it touches, including the prophetic vocation, Israelite expectations about Assyria, and Israel's claim that God is merciful. The book is quite serious theologically—make no mistake about that—but it asks that its readers be sophisticated enough to read beneath the surface meaning of the narrative.

Almost everything in the book of Jonah is hyperbolic or understated. Many prophets offer an initial objection when they are called by God. Moses, Isaiah, and Jeremiah all raise objections and need to be convinced (see Exodus 3, Isaiah 6, and Jeremiah 1). But when Jonah is commissioned to prophesy to Nineveh, he doesn't just object, he runs screaming in the other direction. Half of the book is about his concerted attempts to avoid his prophetic commission! When God sends a storm that threatens to destroy the boat in which Jonah is traveling, the captain finds the prophet snoring in the hold, completely oblivious to the mortal danger. When asked who he is, Jonah blusters, "I am a Hebrew. I worship the LORD, the God of heaven, who made the sea and the dry land" (Jonah 1:9). This is ironic since, far from worshiping God, he has been fleeing God. The mariners are idolaters ("each cried to his god," 1:5), yet when they try their best to avoid having to throw Jonah into the sea, they prove themselves to have more moral integrity than the narcissistic Jonah.

More irony is afoot when Jonah is swallowed by a large fish and prays to God from his fishy place of confinement. Jonah 2 is modeled on a standard psalm of thanksgiving such as we find in the book of Psalms. But the "psalmist" is being parodied here. Many readers have noticed that the imagery of waves closing over the psalmist's head is normally used in psalms metaphorically, as a figure for emotional distress. Here, Jonah is mouthing the same trope but meaning it quite literally. Jonah sings of his praise for God's deliverance before he is actually delivered, which seems to be manipulation on his part. His bold acclamation, "Deliverance belongs to the LORD!" is ironic on at least three levels. First, it turns out that Jonah is angry about prophesying to Nineveh precisely because he doesn't want them to repent so that the LORD will deliver them. Second, deliverance may belong to the LORD, but in this case it is none other than the LORD who got Jonah into these dire straits in the first place. And third, how can Jonah claim to know anything about the LORD when he has been running away from God throughout the story? Interpreters have suggested that when the fish finally spews Jonah out on dry land, it is because the fish is nauseated at the hypocrisy of Jonah's prayer!

Fresh ironies await the reader in Nineveh. Jonah delivers his message in the most begrudging way possible. He spits out tersely, "Forty days more, and Nineveh shall be overthrown!" (only five words in the Hebrew). Yet the effect on the Assyrians is astonishing. Jonah's brief, irritable prophetic word is miraculously effective, and everyone in Nineveh immediately repents, fasting and donning sackcloth. (That even the animals have to fast and wear sackcloth is high satire.) Israel had refused to heed the prophets generation after generation, with catastrophic results. But Nineveh, the huge capital city of one of Israel's cruelest enemies, needs only to hear five words from the bedraggled Jonah in order to repent of "their evil ways and . . . the violence that is in their hands" (Jonah 3:8). And God does refrain from punishing them. Jonah scowls, "I knew that you are a gracious God and merciful, slow to anger, and abounding in steadfast love, and ready to relent from punishing" (4:2). He sulks, and God scolds him for being angry.

What is Jonah about? This question has been debated for many centuries. Some readers say it is about God's showing mercy to all, even the repugnant Assyrians. But that reading is the "straight" reading—the surface meaning—of a book that is thoroughly ironic, so it can be only part of the truth at best. Others suggest that the book shows God's sovereignty over all creation. True enough, but that reading does not account for the specific ironic twists and turns of the narrative. Clearly, the book of Jonah parodies both the prophet and the psalmist. As prophet, Jonah is reluctant, oblivious, and effective only in spite of himself. As psalmist, Jonah is narcissistic, unskilled in the appropriate use of metaphor, and manipulative. Yet Jonah may be sympathetic in the final analysis, for all along he has been aware of a crucial theological incongruity: God may be a God of deliverance for the Assyrians, but God does not show mercy to Israel in 721 or to Judah in 586. No wonder Jonah is resentful!

God is merciful, when God chooses to be. There is no escaping from that truth. But we don't necessarily have to sing it in tones of earnest praise. The book of Jonah gives us permission to proclaim God's mercy in tones of bitterness and anger. For readers of Scripture whose lives are marked by suffering or trauma, that may end up being a profound gift.

Nahum

The book of Nahum ranks with Obadiah as a most troubling witness to ancient Israel's thirst for vengeance against its enemies. Nahum is memorable for its relentless tone of spiteful glee about the fall of Nineveh in 612. Assyria was a particularly cruel foe, to be sure. The Assyrians were renowned not only for large-scale deportations of conquered peoples, but for maiming enemies. They led away captives by means of ropes attached to hooks driven into their faces—horrifying stuff.[4] The prophet Nahum evokes brilliantly the terror that Assyrian forces would have struck into the hearts of their adversaries. Addressing Nineveh, he cries, "Ah! City of bloodshed, utterly deceitful, full of booty—no end to the plunder! The crack of whip and rumble of wheel, galloping horse and bounding chariot! Horsemen charging, flashing sword and glittering spear, piles of dead, heaps of corpses, dead bodies without end—they stumble over the bodies!" (3:1–3).

Perhaps Nahum intends to raise the spirits of Judeans rather than taunt the actual Assyrians, who might not have been listening. But ethically speaking, we nevertheless must balk at this violent rhetoric. Resisting Nineveh's cruelty is one thing. But saying that God will effectively rape and defile the city is another ("I am against you, says the LORD of hosts, and will lift up your skirts over your face. . . . I will throw filth at you and treat you with contempt, and make you a spectacle," Nah. 3:5–6). Violent rhetoric deforms the spiritual imaginations of those who hear it and those who utter it. We can certainly celebrate the larger point of Nahum, that no earthly malevolent power can stand against God's righteous judgment. But this is one biblical book that is best read in conversation with stories that speak of God's mercy. Jonah may want to hear Nahum, but Nahum also needs to listen to Jonah.

Habakkuk

In Habakkuk we see the prophet as sentinel, looking to God for an answer to the anguished question of how long God's people must suffer violence. "Justice never prevails" and "the wicked surround the righteous" (Hab. 1:4). Habakkuk initiates a dialogue with God, and the book unfolds in a fascinating dynamic of speech and counterspeech, silence and agonized cry. Habakkuk asks how long he will cry to God unheard. God answers that God is rousing a terrifying army of Chaldeans, who will sweep through the land bent on violence. Is this meant to silence the prophet? If so, it does not succeed. Habakkuk asks again: Why does God remain silent in the face of wickedness? And God answers that a vision of the end-times is to be written on a tablet, preserved until it is time for its fulfillment. The ambiguity in God's response leads the prophet to elaborate. Surely the arrogant will not endure, the wicked will themselves be plundered, the unrighteous will be "sated with contempt instead of glory" (2:16). Not content to wait meekly, the prophet derides the foolishness of those who worship idols.

And then he falls silent before the power of God. "The LORD is in his holy temple; let all the earth keep silence before him!" (2:20). This may have been the original ending of the book of Habakkuk, for we have found a commentary on Habakkuk among the Dead Sea scrolls that contains only Habakkuk 1 and 2.[5] What a powerful ending that would have been! The prophet has cried out to his God and has heard God's response that he must "wait" (2:3). The prophet wrestles a bit longer, but finally yields to the ineffable power of the holy God. All the earth must keep silence before the LORD. Commentator Francis I. Andersen offers insight into the ironic play around silence here. "The whole matter began with the frantic prayers of the prophet to his silent God. Now the whole world is reduced to silence before the majesty of Yahweh," Andersen says, and he suggests that this silence may include both the "dumbstruck horror" of God's foes and the "hushed reverence" of God's people.[6] If Habakkuk 2:20 was the original ending of the book, the audience would hear the silence at the end of the book as an invitation to encounter the presence of God. Stunning! When we read Habakkuk devotionally, we might pause for prayer at that moment in the text.

What, then, does Habakkuk 3 add to the book? Stirring words of praise for God as Divine Warrior. In ancient times, God strode forth as a cosmic warrior to save God's people, shattering mountains and striking terror into the hearts of Israel's enemies.[7] The unspoken here is that this warrior God can save the people once again. So Habakkuk continues to wait for his God. Despite famine and deprivation, the prophet sings that he will "rejoice in the LORD," and "exult in the God of my salvation" (3:18). His beautiful prayer leads us into the deep silence of worship, to that place where we can know that no matter what, God is our strength (3:19).

Zephaniah

This poetic book offers us a condensed and powerful meditation on the eschatological Day of the LORD. Zephaniah draws on other prophetic traditions to make a unique point. The Day of the LORD will not only be a "day of darkness and gloom" (Zeph. 1:15). God has prepared an eschatological sacrifice, and the offering will be none other than the guests whom God has consecrated! The silence of Habakkuk is elaborated here. Zephaniah's command, "Be silent before the Lord GOD!" (1:7), is a call to the muteness of horror. Zephaniah rebukes those who say that God is irrelevant, who murmur, "The LORD will not do good, nor will he do harm" (1:12).

Repentance is yet possible. The opening verses of Zephaniah 2 summon an unnamed "shameless nation" to seek the LORD, seek righteousness, and seek humility. Irony lurks in the ambiguity here. The "shameless nation" may be the enemies of Israel (Philistines, Moabites, Ammonites, Ethiopians, and Assyrians), all of whom will be obliterated by God's wrath. But the audience cannot be sure that is what Zephaniah means. If Israel identifies itself with the shameless nation, it will convict itself of sin, yet therein lies its only chance of survival. Another suspenseful moment of ambiguity sheds light on that first uncertainty. The prophet excoriates an unnamed city in 3:1: "Ah, soiled, defiled, oppressing city! It has listened to no voice; it has accepted no correction." Israel may be tempted to think this is still part of Zephaniah's invective against enemies, but no. The target comes into terrifying focus as Jerusalem: "It has not trusted in the LORD; it has not drawn near to its God. . . . The LORD within it is righteous" (3:2, 5). As it turns out, God has "cut off nations" and "laid waste their streets" (3:6) in order to instruct Jerusalem in the need for repentance.

God will punish those who are arrogant and unjust (3:8–13). By now we realize that God means the wicked in all the world, including those among God's own people. God will leave a remnant, the "humble and lowly" (3:12), and they shall rejoice in their loving God (3:14–20). The central claim of this short book, wrought with artistic use of ambiguity and irony, is that only those who are humble and penitent can experience God as a God of salvation. Thus an invitation is extended to every reader of Zephaniah: seek the LORD in humility, and you will know the joy of God's salvation.

Haggai

Haggai drives home the importance of rebuilding God's Temple. The book's chronological notices locate the prophet's ministry very precisely, between August 29 and December 18, 520 BCE. We surmise from Haggai 1 that work on the Temple was slated to start but perhaps had been stalled. As long as God's house is not cared for, God's people cannot prosper. "Is it a time for you yourselves to live in your paneled houses, while this house lies in ruins?" Haggai roars. Nothing the people do will succeed until they have committed themselves to honoring God's sanctuary. Haggai 2:1–9 reflects a later stage in the reconstruction process. The Second Temple may not look as glorious as Solomon's Temple, but the people should not fear, for God says, "My spirit abides among you." God will ensure that the wealth of all the nations will flow to Zion, enhancing both the prosperity of the people and the splendor of the rebuilt Temple (2:5–9). God promises blessing "from this day on" at a later date (2:18), likely indicating that the cornerstone has been laid or a foundation consecration ceremony has taken place. The Temple would not be completed for another five years, but the fortunes of the people would improve immediately.

Today the Temple lies in ruins, destroyed by the Romans in 70 CE. So faithful Jews seek to please God by the study of the Scriptures and by prayer, rather than by means of sacrifices. Christians have come to understand the Temple through the redeeming work of Christ (Heb. 9). We are called to work continually toward the upbuilding of the spiritual edifice of the church. For indeed, the congregation of believers is knit together with "Christ Jesus himself as the cornerstone. In him the whole structure is joined together and grows into a holy temple in the Lord, in whom you also are built together spiritually into a dwelling place for God" (Eph. 2:20–22).

Zechariah

This book offers a blend of eight fantastic visions and oracles of the prophet Zechariah (chaps. 1–8, known as "First Zechariah") and a collection of more disjointed oracles that make no mention of the prophet and are composed in a strikingly different poetic style (chaps. 9–14, "Second Zechariah"). The visions confirm that God plans wonderful blessings for God's people and for Jerusalem under the anointed leadership of the high priest Joshua and the governor Zerubbabel. The later oracles prophesy doom and restoration on a vast, even cosmic scale.

Zechariah's visions are magnificent. Divine messengers riding horses, punitive horns, a golden lampstand, a flying scroll, a woman named Wickedness sitting in a basket, four heavenly chariots—all these and more populate Zechariah's storytelling about the future of Israel. The Temple will be rebuilt and the cities of Judah will "overflow with prosperity" (first vision). Enemy nations that had defeated Judah and deported its population will be struck down (second vision). God will be a "wall of fire" protecting Jerusalem and its bustling crowds of people and animals (third vision). Jerusalem's high priest, filthy with priestly corruption or with soot from being tested by the fire of adversity, will be clothed in clean garments; a messianic figure will step forward, and God will "remove the guilt of this land in a single day" (fourth vision). Angelic surveillance agents ("the eyes of the Lord") will roam the earth as the Temple is rebuilt (fifth vision). A curse will cut down those who steal or swear falsely, thus enforcing Torah obedience within the community of the faithful (sixth vision). A secured basket containing a woman who represents Wickedness will be taken to the land of Shinar—that is, Babylon—in order to cleanse Judah of its iniquity (seventh vision). And four divine war chariots go out on patrol, guaranteeing peace to the ends of the earth (eighth vision).

Scholars continue to debate various issues involved in interpretation of the visions. But the overarching theological perspective is clear. The beloved sacred space of Jerusalem is at the center of a cosmos over which God has dominion. Neither the predations of enemies nor the threat of immorality from within can harm the restored faith community. Judah will be extravagantly blessed when the people center their common life around worship of God in the rebuilt Temple (chap. 8).

The oracles in Second Zechariah pronounce judgment on foreign nations and Judah's corrupt leaders, invite Zion to rejoice in her victorious God, and speak of a time when the survivors of the devastated nations will make a pilgrimage annually to Jerusalem to worship the God of Israel. The closing images of the book promise that all of life will be sacred to God. That (war)horses' bells will be inscribed "Holy to the LORD" (14:20) suggests to commentators Carol and Eric Meyers that even war itself will be brought under the dominion of the God of peace.[8] Mundane cooking pots will be as holy as the specially consecrated Temple vessels (14:21), so holiness will permeate every aspect of life. All our living will be an expression of the holiness of God! While we await the fulfillment of this beautiful oracle, we may hear in the closing words of Zechariah a fitting prayer: "All our meals and all our living make as sacraments of thee."[9]

New Testament writers take up prophecies from Zechariah at key moments in their narration of Jesus' ministry. When Jesus enters Jerusalem in triumph, Matthew and John quote Zechariah 9:9, "Look, your king is coming to you, humble, and mounted on a donkey, and on a colt, the foal of a donkey" (Matt. 21:4–5; John 12:14–15). When Jesus predicts that the disciples will desert him at the Garden of Gethsemane, he quotes Zechariah 13:7, "I will strike the shepherd, and the sheep of the flock will be scattered" (Matt. 26:31; Mark 14:27). And John quotes Zechariah 12:10, "They will look on the one whom they have pierced," to make the point that the crucifixion of Jesus is a fulfillment of prophecy (John 19:37).

Drawing on the vision of peace that Zechariah offers, we may acclaim Christ as the Prince of Peace. And surely Zechariah joins his voice to ours when we pray as Jesus taught us, "Thy kingdom come."

Malachi

This prophetic book was written after Haggai, because the Temple worship has clearly begun again and has become corrupt, according to Malachi. He rages about ritual and ethical misdeeds. Priests are offering animals for sacrifice that are blind, lame, or sick, a flagrant violation of Torah stipulations. For an animal to be acceptable, "it must be perfect; there shall be no blemish in it" from disease, injury, or genetic defect (Lev. 22:21–25). To offer less is to profane God's holy name (Lev. 22:32). Priests should teach the people, but these priests have misled the worshipers, causing many to stumble (Mal. 2:7–8). God's people have been "faithless to one another" as well, ignoring covenant prohibitions against marrying foreign women and engaging in divorce in order to hide infidelity (2:10–16). God's people finally have the opportunity to worship aright in the glorious rebuilt Temple, but their hearts are far from God.

A hallmark of Malachi's style is to hammer his audience with outraged rhetorical questions.

"If I am a father, where is the honor due me?" (1:6)
"When you offer blind animals in sacrifice, is that not wrong?" (1:8)
"Shall I accept that [viz., an inadequate offering] from your hand?" (1:13)
"Have we not all one father? Has not one God created us?" (2:10)
"Who can endure the day of his coming? Who can stand when he appears?" (3:2)
"Will anyone rob God?" (3:8)

Where Amos uses rhetorical questions with subtlety to entrap his audience, Malachi wields them as a club to bludgeon his listeners. Judgment will fall on people and priest alike for their carelessness in ritual, their ethical infractions, and their failure to pay the tithes due the Holy One. The people are deluding themselves that the wicked can prosper, that oppressors and adulterers can escape God's wrath. Not so—God is coming like a refiner's fire!

At the end of his book, Malachi shifts to a series of promises. Those who revere the Lord will have their names written in a heavenly "book of remembrance" (3:16) and will be spared on the day of judgment. They will be beloved of God as children are beloved by their parents. This nurturing image is designed to make the shamed and vulnerable audience long to serve God (3:18).

And the prophet offers us an extraordinary image of salvation: "For you who revere my name the sun of righteousness shall rise, with healing in its wings" (4:2). This term "sun of righteousness" reflects the iconography of a winged solar disk, used in many ancient Near Eastern cultures to represent the power and beneficence of the divine.[10] We see a number of oblique uses of this imagery in the Hebrew Scriptures, for example in Psalm 84:11, "The LORD God is a sun and shield; he bestows favor and honor." The "sun of righteousness" image has become familiar to Christians because of its appearance in the Christmas hymn "Hark! The Herald Angels Sing," written by Methodist leader Charles Wesley (1707–88).[11] In the hymn, Malachi's prophecy is applied to Christ:

> Mild he lays his glory by,
> born that we no more may die,
> born to raise us from the earth,
> born to give us second birth.
> Risen with healing in his wings,
> light and life to all he brings,
> hail, the Sun of Righteousness!
> hail, the heaven-born Prince of Peace!
> Hark! the herald angels sing
> glory to the newborn King!

Finally, Malachi exhorts believers to observe the Torah and promises that God will send Elijah to reconcile the faithful before the Day of the LORD. These verses conclude the prophetic corpus in the Hebrew Scriptures, and they conclude the entire Old Testament in the Christian Bible. Early Christian writers saw the fulfillment of these verses in the person of Christ, for Jesus says that he has come "not . . . to abolish the law or the prophets . . . but to fulfill" them (Matt. 5:17–18), and Jesus' transfiguration is attended by both Moses and Elijah (Matt. 17:1–8; Mark 9:2–8; Luke 9:28–36).

By invoking Moses and Elijah in his closing words, Malachi invites us to know God in disciplined practices of obedience and in the prophetic witness of Scripture. Who can endure the day of God's coming (Mal. 3:2)? Perhaps we can, if we bow before the God who thundered on Sinai and who thunders still in the words of the prophets.

Questions for Discussion

1. If your faith community is a spiritual edifice, which parts need repair or refurbishing? Which parts are well constructed and strong?
2. Do you tend to wait quietly for God (Habakkuk), invite the faithful into new visions of God's purposes (Zechariah), or challenge hypocritical believers (Malachi)?
3. Would you say that the Old Testament prophets "predict Christ"? Why or why not?

Notes

Chapter 1: What Is a Prophet?

1. The phrase "speak truth to power" comes from a 1955 document created by Quaker study groups for the American Friends Service Committee, *Speak Truth to Power: A Quaker Search for an Alternative to Violence: A Study of International Conflict Prepared for the American Friends Service Committee*. The document provides a pacifist analysis of American military culture and proposes an alternative politics of nonviolence. William Sloane Coffin took up the saying "speaking truth to power" more generally in his public ministry and in his writings. In his last book, *Credo* (Louisville, KY: Westminster John Knox Press, 2005), 63, 146, he uses the phrase to describe what the biblical prophets did in their calls for justice.
2. See Flavius Josephus, *Antiquities of the Jews* 10.11.
3. See Wilda C. Gafney, *Daughters of Miriam: Women Prophets in Ancient Israel* (Minneapolis: Fortress Press, 2008).
4. Abraham J. Heschel, *The Prophets* (New York: Harper & Row, 1962), 19.
5. Walter Brueggemann, *Theology of the Old Testament: Testimony, Dispute, Advocacy* (Minneapolis: Fortress Press, 1997), 625.

Chapter 2: The Early Prophets

1. Critiques of Balaam may be found in Num. 31:16; Deut. 23:4; Josh. 24:10; Neh. 13:2; 2 Pet. 2:15; Jude 11; and Rev. 2:14.
2. See Roy L. Heller, *Power, Politics, and Prophecy: The Character of Samuel and the Deuteronomistic Evaluation of Prophecy* (New York: T. & T. Clark, 2006).
3. Marvin A. Sweeney illuminates the different ways in which the Elijah stories attack various aspects of Baal's supposed

dominance. See Sweeney, *I & II Kings* (Louisville, KY: Westminster John Knox Press, 2007), 209.
4. Ibid., 232.

Chapter 3: Amos

1. Jon Sobrino, *No Salvation Outside the Poor: Prophetic-Utopian Essays* (Maryknoll, NY: Orbis Books, 2008), 24.
2. Jörg Jeremias argues persuasively that this difficult verse contrasts a wilderness time of "ideal fellowship" with God with later reliance on cultic offerings. See Jeremias, *Amos* (Louisville, KY: Westminster John Knox Press, 1995), 101–5. According to Shalom M. Paul, Amos's point is that "the divine-human relationship is not contingent upon the existence of, or obedience to, any elaborate sacrificial system, but solely and uniquely upon an absolute inviolable commitment to an ethical-moral way of life," *Amos* (Minneapolis: Fortress Press, 1991), 193.

Chapter 4: Hosea

1. Ken Stone, *Sex, Honor and Power in the Deuteronomistic History,* Journal for the Study of the Old Testament Supplement Series 234 (Sheffield: Sheffield Academic Press, 1996), 43–44.
2. Many feminist biblical scholars have analyzed the subtle and not-so-subtle ways in which the prophetic marriage metaphor inscribes male coercive power as godly. See Renita J. Weems, *Battered Love: Marriage, Sex, and Violence in the Hebrew Prophets* (Minneapolis: Fortress Press, 1995); Gerlinde Baumann, *Love and Violence: Marriage as Metaphor for the Relationship between YHWH and Israel in the Prophetic Books* (Collegeville, MD: Liturgical Press, 2003); Gale A. Yee, *Poor Banished Children of Eve: Woman as Evil in the Hebrew Bible* (Minneapolis: Fortress Press, 2003).
3. See Lyn M. Bechtel, "What If Dinah Is Not Raped?" *Journal for the Study of the Old Testament* 62 (1994): 19–36.

Chapter 5: Micah

1. See Marvin L. Chaney, "Accusing Whom of What? Hosea's Rhetoric of Promiscuity," in *Distant Voices Drawing Near: Essays in Honor of Antoinette Clark Wire*, ed. Holly E. Hearon (Collegeville, MD: Liturgical Press, 2004), 97–115; and Gale A. Yee, "'She Is Not My Wife and I Am Not Her Husband': A Materialist Analysis of Hosea 1–2," in *Biblical Interpretation* 9 (2001): 345–83.
2. This oracle appears also, with minor variations, in Isaiah 2. Scholars debate whether Isaiah borrowed from Micah or vice versa, or both

books drew on a common source. Likely this oracle is from postex-ilic times (that is, after 586 BCE) and was seen to elaborate in impor-tant ways on the prophetic messages of both Micah and Isaiah, and so the oracle was added to both books.

3. From William Butler Yeats's poem "The Second Coming," first printed in 1920 and published in 1921 in his collection *Michael Robartes and the Dancer*. See *The Collected Poems of W. B. Yeats*, ed. Richard J. Finneran (New York: Simon & Schuster, 1996), 187.

Chapter 6: Isaiah

1. See John F. A. Sawyer, *The Fifth Gospel: Isaiah in the History of Christianity* (Cambridge: Cambridge University Press, 1996), 1–8.
2. Poem "The H. Scriptures II," in *George Herbert: The Complete English Works*, ed. Ann Pasternak Slater (New York: Alfred A. Knopf, 1995), 56.
3. *The Poems of Emily Dickinson*, ed. R. W. Franklin (Cambridge, MA: Belknap Press, 1999), 215.
4. The divine name "Holy One of Israel" comes up twelve times in First Isaiah, eleven times in Second Isaiah, and twice in Third Isaiah. We might add "the Holy God" in Isa. 5:16 and "Holy One of Jacob" at 29:23 as well.
5. Matthew draws on Isa. 7:14 (see Matt. 1:18–25); Luke's incarnation story draws instead on the Song of Hannah in 1 Sam. 2:1–10 (see Luke 1:39–56).
6. Mark R. Gornik, *To Live in Peace: Biblical Faith and the Changing Inner City* (Grand Rapids: Wm. B. Eerdmans Publishing Co., 2003); Samuel G. Freedman, *Upon This Rock: The Miracles of a Black Church* (New York: HarperCollins, 1993).
7. In Isa. 10:22, where the New Revised Standard Version offers "over-flowing with righteousness"—something that could be misunderstood as a positive image—the Jewish Publication Society has translated bet-ter, "retribution comes like a flood!" This is supposed to be a terrify-ing image, as is the case with the similar image in Amos 5:24.

Chapter 7: Jeremiah

1. Seventy is a standard number for ancient Near Eastern cultures, not unlike forty (as, e.g., the Israelites' forty years in the wilderness and Jesus' forty days being tempted in the wilderness). The Babylonian exile did not, in fact, last seventy years, even if we count from the first deportation of Judean elites in 597 rather than from the fall of Jerusalem eleven years later. Nevertheless, Jeremiah's relatively pre-cise oracle proved the authenticity of his prophecy in the minds of biblical writers.

2. Benjamin D. Sommer, *A Prophet Reads Scripture: Allusion in Isaiah 40–66* (Stanford, CA: Stanford University Press, 1998).
3. Ibid., 37. Many significant parallels and wordplays in the Hebrew Scriptures are obscured by English translation. In this example, Jeremiah's noun "attire" comes from the same Hebrew root as Isaiah's verb "to bind on."
4. See Richard B. Hays, *Echoes of Scripture in the Letters of Paul* (New Haven, CT: Yale University Press, 1989), 44–45, 65–66. Paul may also be drawing on Jer. 31 in 2 Cor. 3 (Hays, 128–29).
5. Jeremiah's stature as a poet of lament has been recognized since before the time of Christ. The Chronicler alludes to a lament that Jeremiah sang for fallen king Josiah (2 Chr. 35:25), in a lament literature no longer extant. In addition, the book of Lamentations is attributed to Jeremiah in the Greek translation of Lam. 1:1. The Greek version opens with this sentence: "And it happened, after the captivity of Israel and the desolation of Jerusalem, that Jeremiah sat weeping, and he lamented this lament over Jerusalem." This introduction is not in the Hebrew original and was added later. That Jeremiah wrote Lamentations seems unlikely, but the identification of Jeremiah with Lamentations shows us that the prophet was associated very early with formal expressions of anguish.
6. Poem "Bitter-sweet," in *George Herbert: The Complete English Works*, ed. Ann Pasternak Slater (New York: Alfred A. Knopf, 1995), 167.
7. Walter Brueggemann, "The Costly Loss of Lament," first published in the *Journal for the Study of the Old Testament* in 1986 and reprinted as pp. 98–111 in *The Psalms and the Life of Faith*, ed. Patrick D. Miller (Minneapolis: Fortress Press, 1995).
8. I argue for this reading of Jeremiah in my *Prophecy and Ideology in Jeremiah: Struggles for Authority in the Deutero-Jeremianic Prose* (London: T. & T. Clark, 2003).

Chapter 8: Ezekiel

1. Readers have long raised the question of Ezekiel's mental stability. For a study that frames Ezekiel in terms of refugee studies and takes seriously the possibility of his suffering from post-traumatic stress disorder, see Daniel Smith-Christopher, *A Biblical Theology of Exile* (Minneapolis: Fortress Press, 2002), 75–104.
2. As Joseph Blenkinsopp notes, Ezekiel demonstrates "an extraordinary breadth of learning seen, for example, in his interest in the archaic period of history, his use of mythological themes, and his expertise in the forms and substance of sanctuary law" (in *A History of Prophecy in Israel*, rev. and enlarged ed. [Louisville, KY: Westminster John Knox Press, 1996], 180).
3. See Daniel I. Block, *The Book of Ezekiel: Chapters 1–24*, New International Commentary on the Old Testament (Grand Rapids: Wm. B.

Eerdmans Publishing Co., 1997), 310–14; Moshe Greenberg, *Ezekiel 1–20*, Anchor Bible 22 (New York: Doubleday, 1983), 177.

4. Block argues that the closest we come to such a claim elsewhere in Scripture is Jesus' saying that his body is the true temple (John 2:19–21) and that true worshipers will worship "in spirit and truth" rather than in Jerusalem or in the Samaritan temple on Mount Gerizim (John 4:20–24). See Block, *Ezekiel*, 349–50.

5. Ibid., 436.

Chapter 9: Other Minor Prophets

1. Marvin A. Sweeney, *The Twelve Prophets*, vol. 1 (Collegeville, MN: Liturgical Press, 2000), xxxi–xxxv.

2. James L. Crenshaw, *Joel*, Anchor Bible 24C (New York: Doubleday, 1995), 26. Crenshaw lists twenty-two quotations in Joel from other biblical books on pp. 27–28. Some of the "quotations" might be disputed. For example, it is an open question as to whether Joel or Jonah was written later. Crenshaw's suggestion that the phrase "for . . . in those days and at that time" (Joel 3:1 = Jer. 33:15; 50:4, 20) is traceable to any particular source is debatable. But even so, the list of Joel's allusions remains impressive.

3. William P. Brown, *Obadiah through Malachi*, Westminster Bible Companion (Louisville, KY: Westminster John Knox Press, 1996), 11–12.

4. See Terence Kleven, "The Cows of Bashan: A Single Metaphor at Amos 4:1–3," *Catholic Biblical Quarterly* 58 (1996): 215–27, 225.

5. See Sweeney, *The Twelve Prophets*, vol. 2 (Collegeville, MN: Liturgical Press, 2000), 457. Francis I. Andersen disagrees, citing shared vocabulary and overarching literary structures that suggest the entire book is a literary unity. See his *Habakkuk*, Anchor Bible 25 (New York: Doubleday, 2001), 259–60.

6. Andersen, *Habakkuk*, 256.

7. For another evocative reflection on the ancient tradition of the Divine Warrior striding through the wilderness, see Ps. 68.

8. They point out that the only other item in the Hebrew Scriptures mentioned as being inscribed "Holy to the LORD" is the rosette on the turban of the priest Aaron (Exod. 28:36), and say that since Aaron is the one who may come nearest to God on earth, the horses and the warfare they represent are being "co-opted into the divine realm" in a way that "signifies the termination of warfare" (Carol and Eric Meyers, *Zechariah 9–14*, Anchor Bible 25C [New York: Doubleday, 1993], 480).

9. From the anthem "Draw Us in the Spirit's Tether," written by Percy Dearmer (1867–1938). The tune to which it is often sung in Christian worship is "Union Seminary," composed by Harold W. Friedell (1905–58).

10. Andrew E. Hill writes that the winged sun disk in the ancient Near East "represented the guardianship of the deity, an emblem of divine effulgence as well as protection and blessing for those peoples overshadowed by the 'wings' of the deity" (*Malachi*, Anchor Bible 25D [New York: Doubleday, 1998], 349–50). Alternatively, Sweeney says that an allusion to the Torah as in Ps. 19 "seems to underlie the references to the righteousness and healing capacities of the sun" (*The Twelve Prophets*, vol. 2, 748).

11. The tune generally used for Wesley's text is "Mendelssohn," composed in 1840 by Felix Mendelssohn (1809–47). The words and order of lines here have been altered from Wesley's original text by several hands, including that of George Whitefield (1714–70). The now-familiar harmonization was provided by William H. Cummings (1831–1915).

Further Reading

Blenkinsopp, Joseph. *A History of Prophecy in Israel: From the Settlement in the Land to the Hellenistic Period*. Rev. and enlarged ed. Louisville, KY: Westminster John Knox Press, 1996.

Brueggemann, Walter. *The Prophetic Imagination*. 2nd ed. Minneapolis: Fortress Press, 2001.

Gafney, Wilda C. *Daughters of Miriam: Women Prophets in Ancient Israel*. Minneapolis: Fortress Press, 2008.

Heller, Roy L. *Power, Politics, and Prophecy: The Character of Samuel and the Deuteronomistic Evaluation of Prophecy*. New York: T & T Clark, 2006.

Heschel, Abraham Joshua. *The Prophets*. New York: Harper & Row, 1962.

McKenna, Megan. *Prophets: Words of Fire*. Maryknoll, NY: Orbis Books, 2001.

O'Brien, Julia M. *Challenging Prophetic Metaphor: Theology and Ideology in the Prophets*. Louisville, KY: Westminster John Knox Press, 2008.

Petersen, David L. *The Prophetic Literature: An Introduction*. Louisville, KY: Westminster John Knox Press, 2002.

Wilson, Robert R. *Prophecy and Society in Ancient Israel*. Philadelphia: Fortress Press, 1980.

CPSIA information can be obtained at www.ICGtesting.com
Printed in the USA
LVOW130907010413

326973LV00001B/42/P

9 780664 231781